RIGHT OF PUBLICITY
IN A NUTSHELL®

SECOND EDITION

MICHAEL D. MURRAY
Spears Gilbert Associate Professor of Law
University of Kentucky, J. David Rosenberg
College of Law

WEST
ACADEMIC
PUBLISHING

444 Cedar Street, Suite 700
St. Paul, MN 55101
1-877-888-1330

Printed in the United States of America

ISBN: 978-1-63659-356-2

INTRODUCTION

Right of Publicity Law

The right of publicity encompasses the legal protection of a celebrity's control over his or her personality rights in the celebrity's name, image, or persona. Publicity law has become one of the fastest growing and rapidly developing areas of law in the United States. Of the fifty states and the District of Columbia, only Alaska, North Dakota, and Wyoming have never recognized by statute or in common law a person's right to be free from the unauthorized and unconsented exploitation of their name, image, likeness, or persona under a theory of privacy or publicity law.[1] From its humble origins as a simple privacy tort, right of publicity has grown into a major area of intellectual property law.

The interest and attention we pay to the stars of sports, entertainment, media, and the arts raises the profile of right of publicity issues. To consider one area of human achievement, the most famous athletes typically make many times more in paid endorsements than they make playing their sport. The size and value of the industries that revolve around celebrities make this a very important area of law. Modern business depends on lawyers who have an understanding of right of publicity law.

---

1 *See* the **Appendix**, *infra*, for the breakdown, state by state, of states recognizing either a publicity law theory or privacy law theory, or neither theory.

Right of publicity law also is a worthy area of study for 21st century lawyers and law students because the law is in flux. Even the black letter principles of this area are only a few decades old, and the law is growing and developing at a breakneck pace. It is not sufficient for intellectual property attorneys to have only a passing familiarity with right of publicity law. The entertainment, media, sports, and advertising industries encounter right of publicity issues on a daily basis.

As a lawyer or law student, or a person whose life or business involves the use of celebrities' and athletes' images and personas, this guide will assist you in understanding the legal issues that arise in right of publicity law, the laws and legal standards that apply to answer the issues, and the information needed to make predictions about probable outcomes of right of publicity disputes. This guide is written with the assumption that you most likely do not have any prior knowledge about American intellectual property law or right of publicity law in particular. This is an open guide for the curious.

Using This Nutshell

The purpose of this Nutshell guide is to orient and acclimate you to the structure, public policy, issues, and vocabulary of the area of right of publicity law. Lawyers practicing in the modern world will observe that the economic power of celebrities in the arts, entertainment, and sports fields, and the symbolic, expressive, and monetary value of celebrities' names, images, and personas are implicated in many areas of business and commerce. Thus, the principle target audience of this Nutshell guide is attorneys and business people working in the arts, entertainment, advertising, marketing, news media, and sports promotion and commerce, and law students taking a course in right of publicity law, entertainment law, art law, media law, or an intellectual property survey course.

This Nutshell is designed to be used in the following ways:

- To get up to speed on the biggest issues of right of publicity law, and the black letter law addressing those issues.
- To educate yourself as to your future clients' rights, potential liabilities, and options and opportunities regarding legal problems in right of publicity law. Whether you plan to specialize in entertainment or intellectual property law, or simply want to be available to your firm or law office as an attorney who can take on a novel problem in an exciting and potentially high-profile and high-dollar-value area of your firm's or office's practice, this book will be useful to you. In many instances, right of publicity law has defined rights and responsibilities and created options and opportunities that are not known or fully understood by the average lawyer.
- To provide a vocabulary of legal terms to use when consulting with lawyers, clients, accountants, financial planners, and insurers regarding problems in the arts,

entertainment, advertising, marketing, news media, and sports promotion fields. When you find yourself involved in a matter that turns out to have right of publicity implications, this vocabulary will help you to be an active and helpful member of the team. It will help you to research, understand, and process the information you will need to give advice to the client and recommendations to your associates and superiors.

- To identify existing or potential legal problems in your clients' and your organization's practices. This guide will discuss a variety of areas in which exposure to legal liability or sanctions may present itself as a current or future problem based on your clients' business practices and procedures.

Welcome to the study of right of publicity law!

ABOUT THE AUTHOR

Professor Michael D. Murray is the Spears Gilbert Associate Professor of Law at the University of Kentucky, J. David Rosenberg College of Law. He previously taught at the University of Massachusetts School of Law, the University of Michigan Law School, Valparaiso University School of Law, the University of Illinois College of Law, and Saint Louis University School of Law. He also has taught in China, Italy, and the United Kingdom. Before beginning law teaching, Professor Murray practiced law at Bryan Cave LLP law firm after clerking for U.S. District Judge John F. Nangle in the Eastern District of Missouri. Professor Murray graduated from Columbia Law School (JD, Harlan Fiske Stone Scholar), Loyola University-Maryland (BA, summa cum laude, Whelan Medal), and from Fudan University in Shanghai, China (Grad. Cert.).

Professor Murray is a busy scholar in the areas of right of publicity, copyright, trademark, and many other art law topics. In addition to his law review and journal articles, he is the author of *A Short and Happy Guide to Copyright* (West Academic), and the co-author of *Art Law in a Nutshell* (West Academic), *Art Law Deskbook, First Amendment and Censorship, The Deskbook of Art Law*, and *Art Law: Cases and Materials*. He also is the co-author of the LRW Series of books at West Academic-Foundation Press, which includes *Advanced Legal Writing and Oral Advocacy: Trials, Appeals, and Moot Court*,

Legal Research Methods, and *Legal Writing and Analysis*.

OUTLINE

TABLE OF CASES

References are to Pages

RIGHT OF PUBLICITY

IN A NUTSHELL®

SECOND EDITION

CHAPTER 1

THE CONCEPT OF A RIGHT OF PUBLICITY

Have you ever wondered about the following?

- When can you use a photograph of a celebrity in your own work without the consent of the celebrity?
- When can an organization print or publish a person's name or likeness in connection with reporting or commenting on news or public interest information involving the person?
- What uses of a celebrity name, image, or likeness are fair, and which can land you into a lawsuit and expose you to liability?

This guide will answer all of these questions.

Publication of the name, image, or likeness of a celebrity is a serious business. The exploitation of celebrity entertainers, sports figures, and just plain famous people is a huge business in the United States. At his peak as a golfer, Tiger Woods made approximately 10–15 million dollars a year playing golf and winning tournaments, but simultaneously made ten times that amount licensing his name, image, and good will for the endorsement of a number of companies—including Nike, Buick, Gillette, EA Sports, Titleist, and his own company, ETW Corporation. With that much money tied up in one sports figure, you should understand the motivation to recognize and protect rights in the use and exploitation of a celebrity's name and image. The law has responded by defining and protecting the rights of celebrities to control and protect their valuable personas and a wide-range of their personal attributes from unconsented exploitation.

WHY SHOULD A LAWYER STUDY THE RIGHT OF PUBLICITY?

A lawyer should study the right of publicity because the sports and entertainment industries have grown to be two of the largest and most profitable industries in the country, and these industries rely heavily on the endorsements of celebrity athletes, artists, and entertainers. Athletes, artists, and entertainers who have reached even a modest level of celebrity status rely on the right of publicity to protect their advertising and publicity livelihood. The United States public pays an inordinate amount of attention to celebrities and sports figures, which in turn raises the profile of right of publicity issues. The size and value of the industries that revolve around celebrities make this a very important area of law. Therefore, it is fair to say that modern business depends on lawyers who have an understanding of right of publicity law.

WHAT DOES A RIGHT OF PUBLICITY PROTECT?

The right of publicity protects a person's name, image, likeness, persona, and often their voice or other distinctive characteristics, from unauthorized commercial exploitation by others. The right has been construed very broadly—basically anything that is exploited by the celebrity herself, or calls to mind, or even is associated with the celebrity, can be protected by the right of publicity. Consider the following examples:

Celebrity	What was protected
Johnny Carson (former host of the *Tonight Show*)	The phrase, "Here's Johnny," spoken by Ed McMahon at the start of the *Tonight Show* —*Carson v. Here's Johnny Portable Toilets*, 698 F.2d 831 (6th Cir. 1983)
Bette Midler (singer, performer)	The sound of her singing voice —*Midler v. Ford Motor Co.*, 849 F.2d 460 (9th Cir. 1988)
John Facenda (longtime voiceover announcer for NFL films)	The sound of his announcer voice —*Facenda v. N.F.L. Films, Inc.*, 542 F.3d 1007 (3d Cir. 2008)
Dustin Hoffman (film star)	His appearance as one of the characters he portrayed in *Tootsie* —*Hoffman v. Capital Cities/ABC, Inc.*, 255 F.3d 1180 (9th Cir. 2001)

Celebrity	What was protected
Muhammad Ali (boxer)	His silhouette and moniker of "The Greatest" —*Ali v. Playgirl, Inc.*, 447 F. Supp. 723 (S.D.N.Y. 1978)
Don Newcombe (pitcher for MLB Dodgers)	His high kick windup on the pitcher's mound and his jersey number —*Newcombe v. Adolf Coors Co.*, 157 F.3d 686 (9th Cir. 1998)
Don Henley (singer for the *Eagles*)	His name —*Henley v. Dillard Dep't Stores*, 46 F. Supp. 2d 587 (N.D. Tex. 1999)
Kareem Abdul-Jabbar (college and professional basketball player)	His appearance playing college basketball (under the name Lew Alcindor) —*Abdul-Jabbar v. General Motors Corp.,* 85 F.3d 407 (9th Cir. 1996)
John Dillinger (Depression-era bank robber, FBI's Public Enemy No. 1)	His name and reputation as a machine-gun wielding criminal —*Dillinger, LLC v. Electronic Arts Inc.*, 795 F. Supp. 2d 829 (S.D. Ind. 2011)

Celebrity	What was protected
Ginger Rogers (film star, dancer)	Her first name, "Ginger," and reputation as a ballroom dancer —*Rogers v. Grimaldi*, 875 F.2d 994 (2d Cir. 1989)
Tony Twist (hockey player)	His name and reputation as an "enforcer" —*Doe v. TCI Cablevision*, 110 S.W.3d 363 (Mo. 2003)

The general idea is that persons have the right to control the exploitation of their name and other features of their personality, and a wrong is done when someone usurps that right without permission.

CHAPTER 2

PRIVACY AND PUBLICITY: ORIGIN AND DISTINCTIONS

In the beginning, there was no right of publicity. It is a modern, twentieth century invention of the law. There was no right of privacy, either, until the beginning of the twentieth century. That is not an idle factoid—the right of publicity began its existence as the right of privacy. Later, in the 1950's, the two rights diverged, as recounted in the following history:

NINETEENTH CENTURY EMBARRASSMENT TO TWENTIETH CENTURY EXPLOITATION

America is one of the first if not the first nation to identify personality rights (specifically, privacy rights) as being a legally protectable feature of our persons. The right of privacy is traced to an 1890 law review article written by future U.S. Supreme Court Justice Louis Brandeis and his one-time law partner and former Harvard Law School classmate, Samuel D. Warren.[1] Brandeis and Warren opined that there ought to be a right of privacy to protect the sensibilities and intimacy of the private lives of private people from intrusion by others, particularly the press.

There is a significant folklore about what motivated the two Harvard law alums, Samuel Warren and Louis Brandeis, to write this forward-thinking

[1] Samuel D. Warren and Louis D. Brandeis, *The Right to Privacy*, 4 HARV. L. REV. 193 (1890) (hereinafter "Brandeis and Warren").

article.[2] The history centers on Warren as the most motivated of the two to write about the proper boundaries of privacy, not because of his own fame and popularity, but because of the rampant and unwanted attention paid to the family he married into—the family of Senator Thomas F. Bayard, a United States Senator from Delaware and former candidate for President, who became Secretary of State under Grover Cleveland. Samuel D. Warren, then a Boston attorney, married Mabel Bayard, the senator's daughter, and found himself in a front-row seat in the eye of the storm of prying and unblinking attention of the Nineteenth Century press and gossip machine.

The coverage of his wife's family may not strike the contemporary reader with horror—our rather outrageous 21st century media climate has long since surpassed all bounds of decency and propriety—but if one can image the relatively prim and mundane life of the average 19th century person, and consider that although Warren was an attorney and later a businessman, and his wife was the daughter of a senator who also was Secretary of State (1885–89) and a former presidential candidate, Warren still reckoned himself and his wife to be private people who suffered from catty social rag-sheet chatter.

---

[2] For a comprehensive treatment of the history and folklore, *see* Amy Gajda, *What If Samuel D. Warren Hadn't Married A Senator's Daughter?: Uncovering the Press Coverage That Led to "The Right to Privacy,"* 2008 MICH. ST. L. REV. 35; Dorothy J. Glancy, *The Invention of the Right to Privacy,* 21 ARIZ. L. REV. 1 (1979).

The chatter was both blunt and insensitive. On the occasion of the death of Mabel Bayard Warren's sister, Katherine Bayard, the Washington Post, January 18, 1886, devoted two columns on page one of the paper to cover deeply intimate details of her death, including the suddenness of the onset of a severe heart condition, her maid's shock in finding her in the throes of distress, the doctor's attempts to revive her, including the use of a galvanic battery to attempt to shock Miss Bayard's heart back into order, the delay in being able to notify the Secretary of State Bayard, and the grief that beset the family after Katherine succumbed to her condition.[3]

ngton Post.

AY. JANUARY 17, 1886.

DEATH'S SAD SUMMONS.

MISS KATIE BAYARD STRICKEN BY HEART DISEASE.

The Sad Intelligence a Great Shock in the Social Circles of the City—Miss Cleveland's Reception, Where Miss Bayard Was to Have Assisted, at Once Postponed and the Mansion Closed.

Miss Katharine Bayard, eldest daughter of Secretary of State Bayard, was found dead in her bed yesterday afternoon shortly after 1 o'clock. Heart disease, an affection with which she had been troubled for some years, was the cause of death.

rooms and handsome toilettes of this group of ladies, who but a few minutes before were happily anticipating joining in a ceremonious and pleasant event, and the contrast when their saddened features expressed their grief and shock at the news was certainly impressive.

The sad intelligence traveled quickly through the city, and universal regret was expressed. People who had seen Miss Bayard well and apparently in the best of spirits only the night before could not believe it, and were soon at the Bayard residence, anxious to show their sympathy. Among some of the callers were representatives of the British, Italian, Danish, Argentine, Spanish, Swiss, Belgium, German, French, Brazilian, Japanese, Russian and Swedish and Norwegian Legations; Senator Payne, Mrs. Whitney,

---

[3] *Death's Sad Summons*, Wash. Post, Jan. 17, 1886, at 1.

And when, a remarkably short time later, on January 31, 1886, Mrs. Louisa Bayard, the Secretary of State's wife and mother of Mabel Bayard Warren, also succumbed to death after a sudden descent into a serious and ultimately fatal illness, the Washington Post on February 1, 1886, again devoted two columns on page one of the paper to the reporting of intimate details of the shock, sadness, and grief of the family.[4]

ngton Post.

Y. FEBRUARY 1, 1886.

DEATH OF MRS. BAYARD.

A DOUBLE AFFLICTION FALLS
UPON THE SECRETARY OF STATE.

Her Demise Due to Congestion of the
Brain, Hastened by Her Daughter's
Death Two Weeks Ago—The Cabinet
Officers to Attend the Funeral.

Mrs. Louisa Lee Bayard, wife of Secre-
tary of State Bayard, died yesterday morn-
ing at half past eight o'clock, of congestion
of the brain, at her residence, 1413 Massa-
chusetts avenue. In the second time in
the brief space of two weeks death has
laid its hand upon the household of the
Secretary. First he saw his eldest and
beloved daughter stricken down in the
flush of her womanhood without a mo-
ment's warning; now the desolate home
sorrows anew for the wife and loving
mother, who could not rally under the
blow which had fallen upon her.

The news of Mrs. Bayard's demise
spread rapidly throughout the city. In a
measure the public had been prepared for

had often championed a weak cause from
what she considered to be merely a sense
of justice. Her sedentary life made her
an omnivorous reader, and she read
books of a solid nature rather than the
works of writers of modern fiction.

The death of Mrs. Bayard will have
a marked effect on the social festivities
at the Capital. It closes in absolute
mourning, for a week which promised to
be unusually gay, the White House and
the houses of the Cabinet Ministers, and
withdraws from society the President and
Miss Cleveland, the members of the Cab-
inet and their families. On the announce-
ment of the sad event yesterday, the
President directed the immediate recall
of the invitations for the State
dinner to the Supreme Court, which
was to have been given Thursday
evening, and Secretary and Mrs. Endi-
cott withdrew their invitations for a
Cabinet dinner on Friday evening.
Miss Cleveland will not be at home to
callers during the week, and her Satur-
day afternoon reception will be aban-
doned. Secretary and Mrs. Whitney had

[4] *Death of Mrs. Bayard*, Wash. Post, Feb. 1, 1886, at 1.

The coverage of Mrs. Louisa Bayard's death was both rudely frank and deeply intrusive, going well beyond public expressions of sympathy and grief to details of private matters that intruded into the family's private grief and dignity, including Mrs. Bayard's failing health and "invalid" status; her weakness and delirium as the end neared; her falling into a coma that preceded her demise; the appearance of her casket; and the open grief of family members at her graveside. The article even callously commented on the negative effect that her demise would have on the "social festivities at the Capital."[5]

Warren appears to have been incensed by this and other examples of intrusive and insensitive gossip that affected his family and in-laws, as reflected in a key paragraph of the article, which states:

> The press is overstepping in every direction the obvious bounds of propriety and of decency. Gossip is no longer the resource of the idle and of the vicious, but has become a trade, which is pursued with industry as well as effrontery. To satisfy a prurient taste the details of sexual relations are spread broadcast in the columns of the daily papers. To occupy the indolent, column upon column is filled with idle gossip, which can only be procured by intrusion upon the domestic circle . . . [causing] mental pain and distress, far greater than could be inflicted by mere bodily injury. . . . When personal gossip attains the dignity of print, and crowds the space available

---

[5] *Id.*

> for matters of real interest to the community, what wonder that the ignorant and thoughtless mistake its relative importance. Easy of comprehension, appealing to that weak side of human nature which is never wholly cast down by the misfortunes and frailties of our neighbors, no one can be surprised that it usurps the place of interest in brains capable of other things.[6]

These sentiments motivated Warren and Brandeis to write the 1890 law review article, *The Right of Privacy*.[7] Lawyers who are not judges and not legislators rarely get the chance to actually write the law on any topic, but Warren and Brandeis came close. They collected cases on various aspects of laws that protect people in their personal lives and worked against private intrusion, and constructed from that the parameters of a new right that could be vindicated as a legal claim. What we think of as the right of privacy is distinctly traced to Warren and Brandeis's law review article.

A FAILED CLAIM FOR EMBARRASSMENT AND SHAME LEADS TO NEW YORK'S STATUTORY PRIVACY LAW

A little over a decade after Warren and Brandeis's article, a woman attempted to litigate a common law claim for "violations of her privacy" in a New York state court. The woman, Abigail Roberson, a minor living in Rochester, N.Y., was embarrassed because

---

[6] Warren & Brandeis, *supra* note 1, at 196.

[7] *Id.*

the Rochester Folding Box Company had placed a photograph of Miss Roberson's head on advertising and trade dress for Franklin Mills Flour. Friends and neighbors scorned and ridiculed her for this event (again—you have to think of early 1900's social mores regarding appropriate behavior of modest young women, not the free-for-all, selfie-obsessed, internet narcissism of today). Roberson had sat for the original photograph in a photographer's studio, but was not informed of and did not consent to the use of her photograph for commercial advertising.

Finding a remedy in the law or in equity for her wrong (embarrassment, disgrace, and emotional distress that manifested itself in physical illness caused by this unwanted exposure) proved to be difficult. Roberson's lawyers, obviously inspired by Warren and Brandeis' article, brought an action asking the New York courts to recognize a common law right of privacy that would prevent the unwanted and unauthorized exploitation of her image and likeness. The argument worked at the trial court and Appellate Division level, which both recognized a common law right of a living person to be free from the unconsented exploitation and public display of that person's likeness, especially in commercial advertising and trade; this was held to be a natural right whose injury demanded a remedy.[8] But the high court of New York, the New York Court of Appeals, by a 4 to 3 margin, did not agree with the lower courts and reversed Roberson's victory.[9]

Readers familiar with the development of the common law and principles of equity in United States courts will know that in the absence of a precedent, the courts will look to analogous situations where claims were entertained in the courts and remedies (damages, injunctions, and other forms of relief) were awarded to claimants. The question for the Court of Appeals was, what was this new right, and to what established claims was it analogous?

The lower courts referred to the right as a "right to be left alone," but even with this vague designation, there was precious little precedent regarding the

---

[8] *See Roberson v. Rochester Folding-Box Co.*, 32 Misc. 344 (Monroe Cnty. 1900), *aff'd*, 64 A.D. 30 (4th Dept. 1901).

[9] *Roberson v. Rochester Folding Box Co. and Franklin Mills Flour Co.*, 64 N.E.442 (N.Y. 1902).

topic of protecting personal seclusion and the sanctity of activities in a person's private life. What little precedent existed, Roberson's facts did not fit well, because her claim did not arise from an invasion of her private seclusion or the sanctity of her home; she posed for the original photograph in a photographer's studio because she and her boyfriend wanted to have a portrait of the plaintiff for their own use. Her complaint was not for libel—the photograph was a fair and attractive likeness of the plaintiff. The photograph did not portray her in a false light; the facts make no mention of whether Miss Roberson had a moral or religious objection to the use of flour or personally opposed the business operations of the defendants. She merely objected to being an unwitting part of a huge commercial advertising campaign. Finding no precedent and no concrete analogous right recognized in the law, the Court of Appeals reversed Roberson's claim.

The dissenting opinion in the case echoed the trial court and Appellate Division opinions in asserting the general rule that there should be no wrong done to a person for which equity cannot provide a remedy. The dissent argued that this principle should have been extended to remedy the modern wrong of unwanted photographic exploitation of a person's image or likeness.

Although her court case failed, Abigail Roberson got the last word, at least in principle. Her failed suit caused a public outcry that was well-covered in the press, and very shortly after her failed action, in 1903, the New York State legislature passed Civil

Rights Law §§ 50 and 51 to regulate the unconsented commercial use of a living person's name, portrait, or picture.[10] Section 50 created a misdemeanor criminal offense and section 51 created a civil claim for damages and injunctive relief. Both sections seek to assist a "person whose name, portrait, picture or voice is used within this state for advertising purposes or for the purposes of trade without the written consent first obtained[.]"[11]

THE COMMON LAW RIGHT OF PRIVACY

By passing Civil Rights Law §§ 50 and 51 in 1903, New York became the first state to protect the right of privacy by statute. But very soon thereafter, in 1905, Georgia became the first state to adopt and apply a common law right of privacy.

In *Pavesich v. New England Life Ins. Co.*,[12] the plaintiff, Paolo Pavesich, asserted a claim for his shame and embarrassment at having his photograph used in a life insurance advertisement. The claimant was not portrayed as the poor and sickly-looking person (on the right) who failed to plan ahead and purchase life insurance ("The man who didn't"), Pavesich was portrayed as the smart and successful "Man who did" buy insurance and was enjoying dividends on his wise purchase. Nevertheless, similar to Abigail Roberson, Pavesich experienced extreme distress from embarrassment for having

---

[10] *See* N.Y. Civ. Rights Law §§ 50, 51 (McKinney 1903), L.1903, c. 132.

[11] *Id.* § 51.

[12] *Pavesich v. New England Life Ins. Co.*, 50 S.E. 68 (Ga. 1905).

been featured in a commercial advertisement without his consent.

The Georgia Supreme Court found that the right to privacy in a situation of appropriation of an image or likeness for commercial purposes was supported by principles of natural law—namely that the "right to withdraw from the public gaze . . . [is] embraced within the right of personal liberty . . . [which] embraces the correlative right of privacy."[13]

The Georgia Supreme Court further justified the right of privacy as a constitutional right of substantive due process, stating:

---

[13] *Id.* at 70.

> The right of privacy within certain limits is a right derived from natural law, recognized by the principles of municipal law, and guarantied to persons in this state both by the Constitutions of the United States and of the state of Georgia, in those provisions which declare that no person shall be deprived of liberty except by due process of law.[14]

Aside from the natural rights of liberty embraced by the court, Pavesich's claim had an element of false light because he in fact had never bought life insurance from the New England Mutual Life Insurance Company of Boston, as represented in the ad copy.

The case described the privacy offense as a tort—a personal injury—entirely separate from any property interest. The court was less concerned with the commercial nature of the exploitation (i.e., in an advertisement for insurance) than the New York legislature in passing N.Y. Civil Rights Law §§ 50 and 51, the provisions of which are predicated on use of a name, image, or likeness in advertising or in trade. The *Pavesich* court found the unconsented depiction of a private, non-public figure in a public manner, such as in a newspaper, to be sufficient grounds for recovery. The court acknowledged that some persons—public officials and those who serve the public in a manner that invites scrutiny into their private dealings and other aspects of their lives that reveal their character and qualifications for their

---

[14] *Id.* at 71.

position—will not be able to prevent exposure of private details of their lives if the details arguably relate to their character or qualifications. The court allowed for other freedom of expression comments and criticisms, too, as a sort of "fair comment" defense to a breach of privacy claim.

Because of its natural rights and substantive due process emphasis, and its designation of the violation of privacy as a personal injury (tort) and not as a violation of property rights, the *Pavesich* opinion is very much the predecessor of modern privacy law, which followed a different path of development in the twentieth century (discussed below, in Chapter 3—The Modern Right of Privacy).

THE TORT VS. PROPERTY DISTINCTION

The tort vs. property distinction regarding privacy and publicity law makes a difference in the operation of laws regulating appropriation of image and persona, and control over unwanted exposure. This chapter is building to an understanding of the modern law of the right of publicity. Tort claims are about personal injury, and the basic categorical narrative of a tort claim is the story of an injury to one's person. With this focus, tort claims address the questions of: Is there a legally cognizable injury? Who caused it? Is that person to blame for causing it—which is to say, is that person liable to the other person for causing the harm, or does the first person have a defense or justification that excuses them from liability?

With privacy concerns, up until the early twentieth century, the answer to the first question was, "No." Breaches of privacy were not a legally cognizable injury. There was no legal remedy for intrusions into privacy. The other questions hardly mattered because there was no claim and no right to bring a legal action until the law changed in the early twentieth century in the United States.

The right of publicity developed as a property claim, and the basic categorical narrative of a property claim is, "Another person is using (or controlling, or exploiting) something that belongs to the plaintiff, and the plaintiff has the exclusive right to control it." With publicity rights, the plaintiff is stating, "My name, my image, my likeness is valuable to me, and I have the exclusive right to decide when and if and by whom it is going to be used. And if I consent to allowing it to be used, I have the right to demand payment for the use."

These two theoretical justifications for the two rights are very different: Privacy claims are personal injury claims. There is little that balances out a personal injury claim—rarely in the law do we say, "Go ahead and injure another person. It's no big deal; they'll get over it. And don't worry about paying them for the injury." There are few public policies and rationales that justify directly injuring another person. Therefore, in tort law claims, the law focuses a great deal of attention on the questions of culpability and liability, so that the law properly assigns the blame and the responsibility to pay for the injuries to the correct person.

Publicity claims are property claims, and the complaint of the celebrity often comes down to money: "The celebrity should have been paid for the use of her name, image, or likeness." The law has come to realize that celebrities are not injured by exposure in the media—they seek out publicity all the time[15]—but they do want to be compensated for the value of their name, image, and persona. This pecuniary focus allows the right of publicity to be balanced by other important rights and public needs—the right of freedom of expression, the right of a free press for news reporting, and the right of comment and criticism are examples of public "goods" (things that are good for the public) that will balance out the right to be compensated for unconsented exploitation.

A FALSE ENDORSEMENT PRIVACY CLAIM

One additional example from the first decade of the twentieth century involved the recognition of an additional justification for recovery for the unconsented use of a name or likeness: that of prevention of unfair competition and protection from consumer fraud. In *Edison v. Edison Polyform*

[15] This finding was the basis of the holding of *O'Brien v. Pabst Sales Co.*, 124 F.2d 167 (5th Cir. 1941), in which a college all-star quarterback could not prevail on a privacy action for publication of his image and name among other football all-stars in a beer company calendar that contained beer advertising. The court found that the information and depiction in the calendar was truthful and not defamatory, and O'Brien regularly consented to widespread publicity, and so the court found that O'Brien had suffered no privacy harm from this particular publicity even though O'Brien did not approve of alcohol consumption.

Manufacturing Company,[16] the defendant perpetrated a product fraud by using without authorization the name and image of the famous inventor, Thomas A. Edison, on a medical compound that was represented to be the neuralgic remedy developed by Mr. Edison. However, the medicine lacked a key ingredient—morphine—and lacked the approval or certification of Mr. Edison himself.

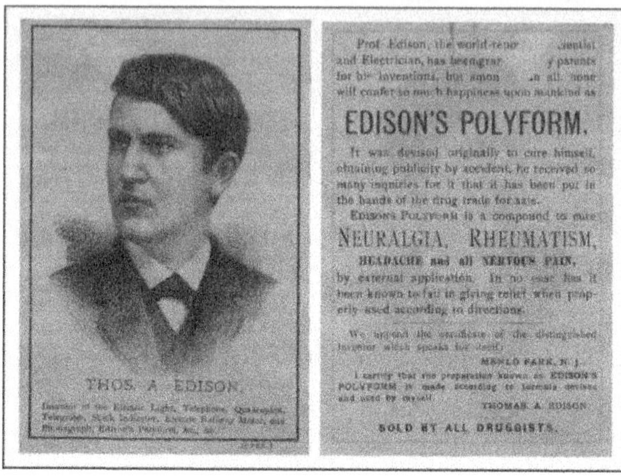

As noted in the advertisement copy, the defendant was so bold as to forge a certification by Mr. Edison, "I certify that the preparation know as EDISON'S POLYFORM is made according to formula devised and used by myself," signed Thomas A. Edison. The court found the defendant liable for falsely appropriating the name and forging the endorsement

[16] *Edison v. Edison Polyform Mfg. Co.*, 67 A. 392, 394–95 (N.J. Ch. 1907).

of a famous scientist and inventor to confuse consumers and fraudulently boost sales, and thus it ushered in a cause of action for "false endorsement" decades before this claim would be codified in federal trademark law under the Lanham Act of 1946.[17] Celebrities and sports figures still may assert false endorsement and false designation of origin claims under federal trademark law today (*see* Chapter 8, False Endorsement and False Designation of Origin, *infra*).

ATHLETES, ACTORS, AND CONTROL OVER PROMOTIONAL RIGHTS

American legislatures and courts slowly developed the law of privacy in fits and starts in the first half of the Twentieth Century, but did not officially separate the tort claims of privacy law from the entirely property-driven claims of the right of publicity until 1953, in the case *Haelan Laboratories, Inc. v. Topps Chewing Gum*.[18] In the five decades between the birth of the right of privacy in New York (1903) and Georgia (1905) and the recognition and enforcement of the right of publicity claim in 1953, athletes in many sports, and Hollywood stars and other celebrities, began to turn the sports and entertainer endorsement market into a valuable sector of the advertising industry.

Sports figures led the way with endorsement deals. As early as 1874, future Baseball Hall of Famer

---

[17] 15 U.S.C. § 1125(a).

[18] *Haelan Laboratories, Inc. v. Topps Chewing Gum, Inc.*, 202 F.2d 866 (2d Cir. 1953).

George Wright of the Boston Red Stockings promoted the Red Stockings Cigar Company. In 1905, baseball great Honus Wagner entered into a highly publicized endorsement deal with J.F. Hillerich & Son Co. to promote Louisville Slugger baseball bats. In 1923, golfer Gene Sarazen signed the longest-running sports endorsement contract in history with Wilson that involved the development of the modern sand wedge; the deal lasted until Sarazen's death in 1999. In 1934, Lou Gehrig was the first athlete to appear on a Wheaties box, while that same year, Elinor Smith, a pilot, was the first female celebrity "champion" to appear on the Wheaties box.[19]

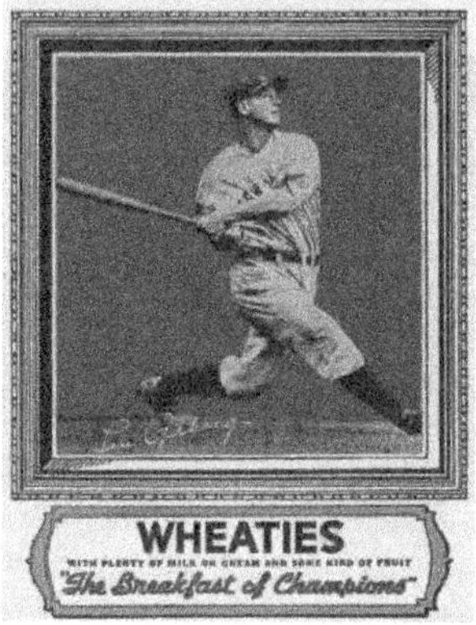

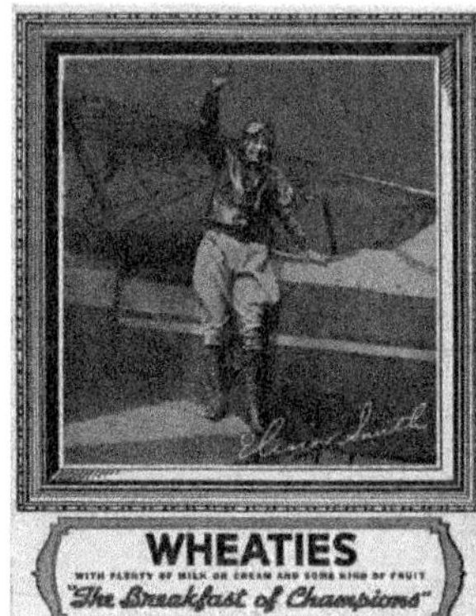

In the 1930's, Mildred Ella "Babe" Didrikson Zaharias, a multisport female athlete who excelled at track and field, golf, baseball, and basketball, became the first nationally-known female athlete to endorse

---

[19] Wheaties boxes in 1934 featuring Lou Gehrig and Elinor Smith.

multiple products, including Dodge cars,[20] golf equipment, and Wheaties.

Hollywood stars were used in promotions, but the strong Hollywood "Studio System" and its industry-standard actor contracts which controlled many aspects of a motion picture actor's career, including in many cases the actor's product endorsements, ensured that most agreements for endorsements were entered into and controlled by the studios. The rise in the film industry's popularity with the invention of "talkies" in 1927 coincided with a massive effort in tobacco advertising, especially for American Tobacco Company's Lucky Strikes, Liggett & Myers's Chesterfields, and R.J. Reynolds' Camel cigarettes. The deal was brilliantly conceived because the motion picture industry was in a position to stylize and glamourize cigarette smoking in motion

[20] Chrysler-Dodge 1933 advertisement featuring "Babe" Didrikson and her 1933 Dodge.

pictures themselves with product tie-ins and on-screen smoking,[21] which the tobacco companies reciprocated by cross-selling advertising of motion picture releases in nationally-distributed tobacco ads. Thus, the endorsements of movie stars were made doubly valuable for the studios and for tobacco companies, if not for the stars themselves who were bound by studio system contracts.

[21] Image of Rita Hayworth promoting the film *Gilda* (1946).

Movie star tobacco ads[22]

[22] Thumbnail images: 1928 advertisement for Lucky Strike cigarettes featuring Al Jolson and referencing his upcoming movie, *The Singing Fool*; 1931 advertisement for Lucky Strike featuring Jean Harlow and her movies, *Hell's Angels, Goldie, and Platinum Blonde*; 1947 advertisement for Chesterfield cigarettes featuring Rita Hayworth and her movie, *Down to Earth*; 1950 advertisement for Camel cigarettes featuring John Wayne as a "popular, handsome, Hollywood star."

By the late 1940's, the tide was turning against the studio system with the antitrust ruling in *United States v. Paramount Pictures, Inc.*,[23] that ended the monopoly power of the studios and forced them to divest themselves of their vertically integrated distribution and movie theater properties. Along with disruption in the movie business in the 1940's, television exerted competition for advertising and actor talent. Actor contracts in Hollywood went from seven-year deals to one-picture deals, and actors gained more rights, but with these rights came the responsibility to negotiate and enforce the rights to their valuable names, images, and endorsements. The law was ready for a change, too.

THE BIRTH OF THE RIGHT OF PUBLICITY PROPERTY LAW CLAIM

The 1953 case of *Haelan Laboratories v. Topps Chewing Gum*[24] was the catalyst of change in the enforcement of publicity rights and not privacy interests. *Haelan Labs* is a case about money, not embarrassment, distress or public shame. The case revolves around a baseball card company's authorized and exclusive use of a name and likeness for baseball trading cards. Plaintiff Haelan Labs, owner of Bowman Baseball Cards, contracted with a baseball player for the exclusive right to use his name and image on baseball cards. Defendant Topps,

---

[23] *United States v. Paramount Pictures, Inc.*, 334 U.S. 131, 156 (1948).

[24] *Haelan Labs., Inc. v. Topps Chewing Gum, Inc.*, 202 F.2d 866 (2d Cir. 1953).

another purveyor of baseball cards, induced the same baseball player to sign a different contract allowing it to use his name and image on baseball cards.[25]

Topps thought it had an airtight defense because the right of privacy was a personal right that was protected by a tort personal injury claim. It was not a proprietary or contractual right that could be assigned or licensed (personal rights are tied to the person of the injured claimant, and thus are not assignable to another person). Therefore, Topps argued the agreement made by the player with Haelan Labs should be construed as a waiver of liability for use of the baseball player's name, portrait, and picture, which otherwise would have been a violation of the player's N.Y. Civil Rights Law

---

[25] Thumbnail-size images of the Bowman-Haelan Labs baseball cards of Wally Moses and Joe Presko, and the Topps baseball card of Tom Poholsky. The players who were involved in dealing with both Haelan Labs and Topps were never identified in the *Haelan Labs., Inc. v. Topps Chewing Gum, Inc.*, 202 F.2d 866 (2d Cir. 1953), opinion, but on remand, these three players—Moses, Poholsky, and Presko—and seven others were identified. *See Haelan Labs., Inc. v. Topps Chewing Gum Co.*, 112 F. Supp. 904, 906 (E.D.N.Y. 1953).

§ 51 rights. A waiver would not give Haelan Labs the right to bring a suit to remedy the privacy violation on its own, and so the case had to be dismissed. The trial court agreed, and dismissed the complaint after a bench trial, but the United States Court of Appeals for the Second Circuit was ready to see the case differently.

The Second Circuit recognized that this dispute had nothing to do with privacy concerns—the baseball player carried out much of his life and livelihood in the public eye. He sought out publicity, rather than avoiding it, and he was not suffering from hurt feelings from the activities of one or both parties who sought to put his name on trading cards. The court recognized that the rights to be protected were economic property rights—a famous figure's valuable, marketable publicity value. The issue here was not a tort claim of who was responsible for personal injuries. It was a property (and contract) law claim regarding which of the two baseball card companies had the right to exploit the image of the player.

The court was ready to place the new right within property law, instead of tort law, and thereafter named it the "right of publicity." The court stated,

> We think that, in addition to and independent of that right of privacy (which in New York derives from statute), a man has a right in the publicity value of his photograph, i.e., the right to grant the exclusive privilege of publishing his picture, and . . . [t]his right might be called a "right of publicity." For it is common knowledge that

> many prominent persons (especially actors and ball-players), far from having their feelings bruised through public exposure of their likenesses, would feel sorely deprived if they no longer received money for authorizing advertisements, popularizing their countenances, displayed in newspapers, magazines, busses, trains and subways. This right of publicity would usually yield them no money unless it could be made the subject of an exclusive grant which barred any other advertiser from using their pictures.[26]

In this manner, the right of publicity as a property law interest and claim was officially endorsed.[27] Meanwhile, the right of privacy as freedom from intrusion into private matters continued. Some state laws, such as N.Y. Civil Rights Law §§ 50, 51, still include both concepts of the rights, privacy and publicity, to be protected within the same law. The concept of a privacy tort, such as false light, harmful publication of private facts, or harmful appropriation of the persona of a private person, carries on in the common law or statutory law of many states (*see* Chapter 3 below). Eventually, the simple distinctions between tort and property justifications for a right of privacy vs. a right of publicity were enriched and expanded (as explained in Chapter 4 below). Federal law does not supersede the field of publicity law,

---

[26] *Haelan Labs.*, 202 F.2d at 868.

[27] In 1954, a renowned expert of copyright law, Melville Nimmer, clarified the recently recognized and endorsed right of publicity. *See* Melville B. Nimmer, *The Right of Publicity*, 19 LAW AND CONTEMPORARY PROBLEMS 203–223 (Spring 1954).

although Section 43(a)(1) of the Lanham Act, 15 U.S.C. § 1125(a)(1), creates a federal remedy for false endorsements or false designations of origin used in connection with the sale of a product that sometimes is used to attempt to vindicate an unauthorized use of a celebrity's name or likeness in commerce or trade (*see* Chapter 8 below).

CHAPTER 3

THE MODERN RIGHT OF PRIVACY

By the end of the 1950's, privacy law in the United States attempted to regulate and prevent the following torts:[1]

- **Invasion of privacy**—physical invasions into the sanctity of the home or the private sphere, causing harm, embarrassment, hurt feelings, or distress.[2]
- **Publication of private facts in a harmful manner**—usually means a prying, snooping, or otherwise questionable acquisition of non-public facts about a private person's private life and affairs, followed by the publication of these facts in a manner that causes hurt feelings, embarrassment, and distress.[3]
- **False light**—publication of private matters in a negligent or reckless manner that causes a false impression about a person.[4] It is

---

[1] These different rights of action were identified by the renowned expert on tort law, Dean William Prosser, in his article, William L. Prosser, *Privacy*, 48 CAL. L. REV. 383 (1960).

[2] *See, e.g.*, *U.S. Dep't of Justice v. Reporters Comm. For Freedom of Press*, 489 U.S. 749, 762 & n.13 (1989); *New Jersey v. T.L.O.*, 469 U.S. 325, 337 (1985); *Griswold v. Connecticut*, 381 U.S. 479, 484–85 (1965).

[3] *Bodah v. Lakeville Motor Express, Inc.*, 663 N.W.2d 550, 553 (Minn. 2003); *Shulman v. Grp. W Prods., Inc.*, 18 Cal. 4th 200, 231–33 (1998), *as modified on denial of reh'g* (July 29, 1998).

[4] *Graboff v. Colleran Firm*, 744 F.3d 128, 139 (3d Cir. 2014); *West v. Media Gen. Convergence, Inc.*, 53 S.W.3d 640, 643–44 (Tenn. 2001).

related to famous dignitary crimes or intentional torts of defamation and slander, but the proof requirements are easier to meet. Slander and defamation require an intentional act, and require proof of reputational damage—called "special damages" in this context. False light requires proof of harm, but it need not be the special damages to one's public reputation that are required in a defamation or slander suit. The elements are: (a) the false light in which the other was placed would be highly offensive to a reasonable person, and (b) the actor had knowledge of or acted in reckless disregard as to the falsity of the publicized matter and the false light in which the other would be placed.[5]

Both publicity and privacy actions also could be used to prosecute the fourth type of tort action:

- **Wrongful appropriation of a *private* person's likeness or persona for commercial purposes**

Both privacy and publicity claims will look to the commercial nature of the exploitation. The motivation to sue and the damages the victim will prove probably will differ in the two kinds of action. In a privacy suit, the claim will be that the use of the plaintiff's image in commercial advertising was

---

[5] Restatement (Second) of Torts § 652E (1977). *See White v. Fraternal Order of Police*, 909 F.2d 512 (D.C. Cir. 1990); *Phillips v. Smalley Maint. Servs., Inc.*, 435 So. 2d 705 (Ala. 1983); *Godbehere v. Phoenix Newspapers, Inc.*, 783 P.2d 781 (Ariz. 1989); *Dodrill v. Arkansas Democrat Co.*, 590 S.W.2d 840 (Ark. 1979).

embarrassing and hurtful, or affected the reputation of the victim in a negative manner. In a publicity claim, the allegation will be that the victim did not consent to the use and that the defendant unfairly enriched himself by taking and using the image without bothering to pay for it.[6]

Lastly, right of publicity claims vindicate the **property** offense of:

- **Wrongful appropriation of a *famous* person's valuable name, likeness, or persona**

The property claim and cause of action reflects the monetary value of a famous person's name, image, or likeness. Famous people live in the limelight, and media exposure is nothing new to them. Publicity in and of itself does not cause hurt feelings or embarrassment. But the celebrity knows her image is valuable, and wants to be paid for uses of her name or image, especially when used in connection with a commercial endeavor or in the advertising of a product or service.[7]

Privacy law branched out in the 1960s in ways that opened up the concept to many, varied situations.

---

[6] *See Zacchini v. Scripps-Howard Broad. Co.*, 433 U.S. 562, 572 & n.7 (1977).

[7] *See* Restatement (Third) of Unfair Competition § 46 (1995); *Hart v. Elec. Arts, Inc.*, 717 F.3d 141, 155 (3d Cir. 2013). Thirteen states recognize the common law privacy law "appropriation" claim in lieu of a right of publicity claim—Colorado, Connecticut, Delaware, District of Colombia, Idaho, Iowa, Kansas, Maine, Maryland, Mississippi, Montana, North Carolina, and Vermont. *See* the Appendix.

Privacy and the sanctity of seclusion of private affairs were used as the basis for the protection of several newly-recognized constitutional civil rights.

In 1965, the Supreme Court decided the case of *Griswold v. Connecticut*[8] which concerned the right to use contraception for birth control in the privacy of one's own home. This personal freedom may not encounter very many challenges in the twenty-teens, but there was enough controversy over the issue as late as the 1960's for states to have put laws into place regulating the right. The *Griswold* opinion changed the state of privacy law from the common law and occasional statutory provisions which protected personal freedom from unwanted intrusion and from certain publications and misconstructions of private facts in actions such as false light. The *Griswold* case looked further afield, and drew support for the concept of personal privacy and personal freedom more broadly in constitutional law.[9]

The *Griswold* Court found support for the protection of personal privacy and personal freedom from "emanations surrounding" the "penumbra" of six amendments to the United States Constitution: the **First Amendment** (freedoms of free exercise of religion, speech, and association), **Third Amendment** (no quartering of soldiers in private homes), **Fourth Amendment** (freedom from warrantless searches and seizures), **Fifth**

---

8 *Griswold v. Connecticut*, 381 U.S. 479 (1965).

9 *Id.* at 484–86.

Amendment (the right to due process, confrontation of evidence, freedom from double jeopardy and self-incrimination, and other protections from being improperly and unfairly incarcerated), **Ninth Amendment** (the protection of unnamed—unenumerated—rights that are retained by the people), and **Fourteenth Amendment** (the guaranty of due process including the rights of the Bill of Rights to persons in all of the states of the union).[10] Justice William Douglas, writing for the court in *Griswold*, argued that the specific rights guaranteed in these six amendments could not be fully enjoyed and realized unless the law recognizes their "penumbras" that have a broader meaning than the original meaning of their original texts.[11] Quartering, for example, was originally meant to address an oppressive government regime, such as that of the British, who forced private citizens to feed and provide lodging for soldiers in their own private homes. Certainly, the right not to have to quarter soldiers by itself would be highly appreciated, but the meaning of the provision was held to be broader. It stood for the general sanctity of a private home, and the understanding that government, in general, has no business snooping into the home unless there is a supervening, compelling reason to do so.

Griswold transformed the concept of privacy from a few small restrictions on intrusion to a broad-based protection of personal autonomy. The courts slowly adapted the *Griswold* ruling to new situations. In *Roe*

---

[10] *Id.* at 484–85.

[11] *Id.*

v. Wade (1973),[12] the Supreme Court held that laws prohibiting a woman's ability to have an abortion violated her fundamental right to privacy (as in personal freedom), and, as such, were unconstitutional.[13] In *Lawrence v. Texas* (2003),[14] the Supreme Court struck down the criminal prohibition of sodomy under state law, once again affirming a personal freedom that typically is undertaken in the privacy and sanctity of a personal home.[15]

Meanwhile, the right of privacy as freedom from intrusion into private matters continued. As noted in the previous chapter, some state laws, such as N.Y. Civil Rights Law §§ 50, 51, still include both concepts of the rights, privacy and publicity, to be protected within the same law. The concept of a privacy tort, such as false light, harmful publication of private facts, or harmful appropriation of the persona of a private person, carries on in the common law or statutory law of many states.

A FALSE LIGHT CLAIM WITHOUT ACTUAL MALICE

The case of *Time, Inc. v. Hill*[16] concerns the reporting of a fictionalized account of a real life dramatic and traumatic event. In real life, the Hill family was taken hostage by escaped convicts from a Pennsylvania prison. The hostages were eventually

---

[12] *Roe v. Wade*, 410 U.S. 113 (1973).

[13] *Id.* at 164–66.

[14] *Lawrence v. Texas*, 539 U.S. 558 (2003).

[15] *Id.* at 578–79.

[16] *Time, Inc. v. Hill*, 385 U.S. 374 (1967).

released without harm or violence. In the fictionalized account by Joseph Hayes, an Indiana family was taken hostage by escaped prisoners from an Indiana prison.[17] The fictional story was considerably more dramatic, with violence done to the father, and threats of violence to the other Hill family members.[18]

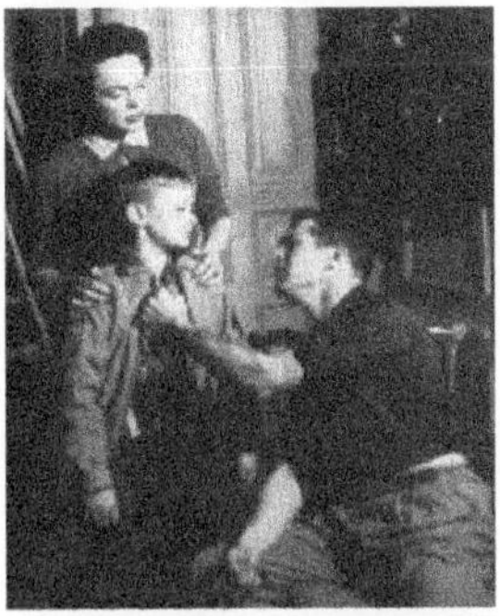

In the stage adaptation, Paul Newman threatens the young son of the family

In the stage adaptation, Paul Newman jeers at Karl Malden, the father

[17] *Id.* at 391–92.

[18] Collage of thumbnail images from the stage production and motion picture promotional material of *The Desperate Hours*, the subject matter of the case, *Time, Inc. v. Hill*, 385 U.S. 374, 391–92 (1967).

In the film adaptation, Humphrey Bogart pistol whips the father, played by Frederic March

High drama in the film adaptation

DAILY NEWS

BANK ROBBERS HOLD FAMILY IN WHITEMARSH PRISONERS;

ACTUAL EVENT, as reported in newspaper, took place in isolated house about 10 miles from Philadelphia. There three convicts from Lewisburg penitentiary held family of James Hill as prisoners while they hid from manhunt. All three convicts were later captured.

TRUE CRIME INSPIRES TENSE PLAY

The ordeal of a family trapped by convicts gives Broadway a new thriller, 'The Desperate Hours'

Three years ago Americans all over the country read about the desperate ordeal of the James Hill family, who were held prisoners in their home outside Philadelphia by three escaped convicts. Later they read about it in Joseph Hayes's novel, *The Desperate Hours*, inspired by the family's experience. Now they can see the story re-enacted in Hayes's Broadway play based on the book, and next year will see it in his movie, which has been filmed but is being held up until the play has a chance to pay off.

The play, directed by Robert Montgomery and expertly acted, is a heart-stopping account of how a family rose to heroism in a crisis. LIFE photographed the play during its Philadelphia tryout, transported some of the actors to the actual house where the Hills were besieged. On the next page scenes from the play are re-enacted on the site of the crime.

The defendant, Time, Inc., owner of Life Magazine, covered the run of the stage play and the announcement of the film version by reprinting news headlines from a newspaper's reporting on the actual hostage taking, and published a photograph taken of the actual house, the former Hill residence, that was the actual site of the hostage crisis. Life even went so far as to stage some "reenactments" of the events of the hostage taking using the actors from the current run of the stage show. The reenactments were not of the actual event, but of the fictionalized account of the event. Life's actions were alleged by Hill to suggest that the fictionalized account was a closely accurate telling of the true facts of the hostage taking event. In fact, it wasn't. Although Hill and his family no longer lived in the Pennsylvania house (they had moved to New York State), Hill still was dogged by the incorrect account in the magazine and the suggestion that the stage play and movie were completely accurate. In Hill's words, the prisoners were not abusive or threatening, they were polite to a degree, and the whole event was not harrowing or suspenseful. Of course, the dramatic fictionalization was both harrowing and suspenseful, and Hill thought the way Life Magazine covered it placed him in a false light.[19] Hill sued in his new home state of New York under the old New York law, the N.Y. Civil Rights Law §§ 50, 51.

The trial court accepted that Hill had suffered injury and sustained his theory of false light. However, on appeal, the Supreme Court of the United States held that the case had to be evaluated in light of the case, *New York Times v. Sullivan*,[20] which had held that news reporting could not be indirectly censored or subjected to after-the-fact liability by state law

[19] *Time v. Hill*, 385 U.S. at 391–93.

[20] *New York Times Co. v. Sullivan*, 376 U.S. 254 (1964).

causes of action such as defamation unless the news outlet was found to show "actual malice" toward the plaintiff.[21] Actual malice requires a showing of intentional falsity or recklessness toward the truth. Recklessness in the law is a significant cut above mere negligence, and the Court found that all that could be said about the way Life reported on the stage and film adaptations of Hill's real life story was that Life was negligent about how it portrayed the events. As a news outlet, albeit of very broadly defined public interest news, Life was protected by the absence of actual malice standard and was held not liable to Hill.

On a historical note, Hill's attorney at the Supreme Court was none other than a former vice-president and congressman from California, Richard M. Nixon, who was in between political gigs, and about to win the United States presidential election in 1968. And the drama of Nixon's presidency far outshined the little hostage crisis of *Time v. Hill*. But that is a story for another time and place.

A MODERN PRIVACY CLAIM OF A PUBLIC FIGURE[22]

In the late 1960's and early 1970's, Jacqueline (Jackie) Kennedy Onassis, the widow of the assassinated president, John F. Kennedy, and a public figure in New York City, was plagued by the attention of paparazzi photographers who strove to

---

[21] *Id.* at 283–84.

[22] *Galella v. Onassis*, 353 F. Supp. 196 (S.D.N.Y. 1972), *aff'd and modified*, 487 F.2d 986 (2d Cir. 1973).

capture every movement in public that she and her children, Caroline and John Jr. (John-John), ever made. The most aggressive of the paparazzi was Ron Galella, who went out of his way to frustrate the movements of the former first family so that he could capture them on film. Galella ran in front of John-John's bicycle, drove a motorboat dangerously close to Jackie while she was swimming, and invaded the children's schools, all in an effort to grab pictures of the Kennedy heirs. He bribed doormen, romanced a domestic worker in the Onassis household, and did everything he could to discover where the family went in town and on vacations.

Galella stalking Jackie Onassis

Galella captures John-John and Jackie riding in Central Park

Galella mocks Jackie by measuring off his distance after a restraining order forced him to stay 25' from her[23]

In the course of the incident where Galella ran in front of John-John's bicycle, Galella was arrested and interrogated by the Secret Service protecting Mrs. Onassis and her children, and his handling by the agents was alleged to be rough. Galella sued the agents and Mrs. Onassis for various torts and civil rights violations. Onassis countersued alleging invasions of privacy and intentional infliction of emotional distress. The downside of the suit for Galella was that the trial judge heavily favored Onassis, he was inclined to recognize none of Galella's claims, and he put into place an injunction preventing Galella from coming near to (within 25

---

[23] (Prior page and this page) Thumbnail-size images of Ron Galella, Jackie Onassis and John Kennedy Jr., the subjects of the case, *Galella v. Onassis*, 353 F. Supp. 196 (S.D.N.Y. 1972), *aff'd and modified*, 487 F.2d 986 (2d Cir. 1973).

feet of) Onassis. He also prevented Galella from selling, publishing, or advertising any of his photographs of Onassis. On appeal, Galella reasserted his basic contention that the First Amendment freedom of press clause prevented Onassis from bringing her claims and from enjoining his activity. The court of appeals agreed in part—the injunction on selling, publishing, or advertising any of his photographs of Onassis was ended. All of the other parts of the injunction remained in effect.

A MODERN PRIVACY CLAIM IN BODILY INTEGRITY

The facts of *Moore v. Regents of the University of California*[24] tell a modern tale of privacy rights in our own bodies and tissues, and these facts sound very relevant to contemporary events and issues in biochemistry, gene science, and genetic engineering. Plaintiff Moore was treated by a doctor at UCLA Medical Center for hairy cell leukemia. In the course of treatment, the doctor took many skin, bone, blood, and sperm samples. Moore didn't mind, until he learned that the doctor was making a cell line out of his cells and intended to patent and profit from it. Moore sued the doctor and the medical center. The case made its way to the California Supreme Court, which held that Moore did *not* have any right in the cells taken in the course of his treatment, nor any financial stake in the cell line that the doctor developed from his cells. The theory pursued by

---

[24] *Moore v. Regents of Univ. of California*, 793 P.2d 479 (Cal. 1990).

Moore was not privacy or even intrusion into bodily integrity, but rather a straightforward action for conversion—which is legal parlance for "theft" in a civil law context. The privacy claim may have fallen short because Moore consented to treatment, and went along with the skin and blood and bone marrow sampling each time the doctor asked for it. However, the court opined that Moore or others in his situation might in proper circumstances bring a claim under the theories of breach of fiduciary duty or lack of informed consent because his physician did not make him fully aware of the uses to which the physician was adapting his cells, and the situation raises at least an argument that the doctor may have breached his fiduciary duty to Moore if the doctor directed treatment in a manner that would allow him to harvest cells and complete his cell line.[25]

NO RELIGIOUS PRIVACY IN A PUBLIC PLACE

The facts of *Nussenzweig v. diCorcia*[26] begin with Erno Nussenzweig walking along an avenue in Manhattan when, without his knowledge or consent, he was photographed by Philip-Lorca diCorcia. Unknown to Nussenzweig at the time, his picture was to become a part of a collection of photographs taken by diCorcia, a professional photographer who surreptitiously took the pictures of a random group

---

[25] *Id.* at 487–97.

[26] *Nussenzweig v. diCorcia*, 11 Misc. 3d 1051(A) (N.Y. Cty. 2006), *aff'd*, 38 A.D.3d 339 (1st Dep't), *certified question answered, order aff'd*, 9 N.Y.3d 184 (2007).

of private citizens as they walked the public streets of this major city. diCorcia waited to take the photograph until the unsuspecting subjects walked across the spot on the sidewalk to which he had pointed his hidden camera and artificially illuminated with small strobe lights. Once diCorcia had enough of the photos, he selected and edited some seventeen of the pictures, one of which was "Head No. 13," the photograph of Nussenzweig,[27] and published them at the famous Pace/MacGill Gallery in New York, in a collection titled, "HEADS."

The photos in the exhibition were 5 feet tall and 3.33 feet wide. diCorcia defended his actions by explaining that, "the artistic expression and commentary [he is]

[27] Thumbnail-size image of Head No. 13 (Erno Nussenzweig), the subject of *Nussenzweig v. diCorcia*, 11 Misc. 3d 1051(A) (N.Y. Cty. 2006), *aff'd*, 38 A.D.3d 339 (1st Dep't), *certified question answered, order aff'd*, 9 N.Y.3d 184 (2007).

making is how wonderful and telling each common, human face is when revealed by large format photography and special lighting. Each face speaks volumes about the human condition, existence, isolation, or the interconnection of all people, even when they are just walking down the street, woolgathering in the most private manner." diCorcia eventually sold for a price of between $20,000 and $30,000 all ten of the copies of "Head No. 13" which he produced. The commercial objective and profitable use of the "HEADS" collection was not disputed. At no time did diCorcia seek or obtain the permission from any of his subjects to take or use these photos.

Nussenzweig is an Orthodox Hasidic Jew and a member of the Klausenberg sect, a group who suffered particular persecution in Nazi-held Europe during World War II. His offense at diCorcia's use of his photograph in this manner was a product of his deeply held personal and religious convictions that such a public or commercial use of his image violates the Biblical prohibition against worship of graven images. After being informed that diCorcia would not voluntarily withdraw "Head No. 13" from exhibition or sale in deference to his request, Nussenzweig sought to protect his right to privacy through legal means.

The problem for Nussenzweig was that the N.Y. Civil Rights Law § 51 has a strong exception for First Amendment speech activities,[28] and the creation and sale of artistic expression is included in this

[28] N.Y. Civ. Rts. Law § 51.

exception. diCorcia asserted this defense of freedom of speech, and in particular, the freedom of artistic expression. New York courts are very generous with artistic expression when it collides with the right of privacy or publicity.[29] The use in art of an image of a person walking along on a public street (as opposed to an image caught by an actual, physical invasion of the photographer into the privacy of a person's home) has a good chance of surviving even a highly sympathetic privacy claim such as Nussenzweig's.[30]

The trial court in *Nussenzweig* granted the exception in favor of the artistic expression of diCorcia;[31] however, on appeal, the case ultimately was disposed of as untimely under the statute of limitations based on the "first publication" rule and the date that Nussenzweig brought his action after the first publication of the photograph.[32] But from the discussion and concurring opinion in the Appellate Division, First Department, and by the New York Court of Appeals opinion, it appeared that the courts were prepared to let diCorcia prevail on his First

---

[29] *See Messenger ex rel. Messenger v. Gruner + Jahr Printing and Pub.*, 706 N.Y.S.2d 52 (Ct. App. 2000); *Foster v. Svenson*, 7 N.Y.S.3d 96 (N.Y. App. Div. 1st Dep't 2015); *Altbach v. Kulon*, 754 N.Y.S.2d 709 (App. Div. 3rd Dept. 2003); *Davis v. High Soc. Magazine, Inc.*, 457 N.Y.S.2d 308 (App. Div. 2nd Dept. 1982); *Simeonov v. Tiegs*, 602 N.Y.S.2d 1014 (Civ. Ct. N.Y. City. 1993). *See also Hoepker v. Kruger*, 200 F. Supp. 2d 340 (S.D.N.Y. 2002) (applying N.Y. Civ. Rts. Law § 51).

[30] *See Foster*, 7 N.Y.S.3d at 96; *Simeonov*, 602 N.Y.S.2d at 1014; *Hoepker*, 200 F. Supp. 2d at 340.

[31] *Nussenzweig v. diCorcia*, 11 Misc. 3d 1051(A) (N.Y. Cty. 2006) (table disposition; opinion on Westlaw).

[32] *Id.*, 38 A.D.3d at 348–49.

Amendment artistic expression defense against the plaintiff's claims under N.Y. Civil Rights Law § 51, if they reached that issue.[33]

In the recent case of *Foster v. Svenson,* the N.Y. Supreme Court Appellate Division, First Department, affirmed the artistic expression defense in favor of a photographer who actually used his camera to zoom in on and depict the lives of persons living in high rise apartments in New York City, with large picture windows the photographer could peer into from another high rise nearby.[34]

---

[33] *Nussenzweig v. diCorcia*, 11 Misc. 3d 1051(A) (N.Y. Cty. 2006), *aff'd*, 38 A.D.3d 339 (1st Dep't), *certified question answered, order aff'd*, 9 N.Y.3d 184 (2007).

[34] *Foster*, 7 N.Y.S.3d at 96.

CHAPTER 4

THEORY AND POLICY SUPPORTING THE RIGHT OF PUBLICITY

The right of publicity was born out of the necessity to allow a more modern view of favorable media exploitation and its value to a certain group that might be identified as celebrities and sports figures to whom the use of their name, image, and likeness is extremely valuable. Often, as noted in the introduction and Chapter 1, the publicity value is more valuable than the compensation received for playing a sport or pursuing an entertainment career. The *Haelan Laboratories, Inc. v. Topps Chewing Gum*[1] case that first recognized and endorsed the property claim of right of publicity was a fairly short opinion, and it spent no time at all exploring the theoretical justifications and public policy support for the new right. It was enough for the Second Circuit to declare that the old privacy claim of "appropriation" was out-of-date and ill-designed for the modern world of celebrities and sports figures for whom publicity was a lucrative business opportunity and a not a matter of embarrassment or personal harm. Therefore, the court created an assignable property interest that could be enforced by the assignee (Haelan Labs in the lawsuit's scenario) to fit the modern promotional endorsement "publicity" model.

---

[1] *Haelan Laboratories, Inc. v. Topps Chewing Gum, Inc.*, 202 F.2d 866 (2d Cir. 1953).

NATURAL LAW AND THE LABOR THEORY

Melville Nimmer's article, *The Right of Publicity*,[2] a year after *Haelan Labs*, explained well what Judge Frank and the Second Circuit had done in the *Haelan Labs* case, and Nimmer spent most of the article explaining why the recognition of a right of publicity was a good idea because other theories for recovery of publicity-type injuries were inadequate. But Nimmer provided one core public policy justification for the newly identified right—a natural law theory that every person should receive the fruits of their labors:

> It would seem to be a first principle of Anglo-American jurisprudence, an axiom of the most fundamental nature, that every person is entitled to the fruit of his labors unless there are important countervailing public policy considerations. Yet, because of the inadequacy of traditional legal theories discussed [previously], persons who have long and laboriously nurtured the fruit of publicity values may be deprived of them, unless judicial recognition is given to what is here referred to as the right of publicity—that is, the right of each person to control and profit from the publicity values which he has created or purchased.[3]

This single theory is fairly simplistic, and it fails to comfortably accommodate the overnight success or

---

[2] Melville B. Nimmer, *The Right of Publicity*, 19 LAW AND CONTEMPORARY PROBLEMS 203–223 (Spring 1954).

[3] *Id.* at 216; *see also* J. Thomas McCarthy, *Melville B. Nimmer and the Right of Publicity: A Tribute*, 34 UCLA L. REV. 1703, 1711 (1987).

"accidental celebrity" of the modern era, or those who are famous for being famous without having expended a lifetime of training in entertainment, the arts, or sports as the labor for reward.[4] Other theories emerged, and by the mid-1970s, there were three espoused by the United States Supreme Court in its only foray into the field of right of publicity, *Zacchini v. Scripps-Howard Broadcasting Co.*[5]

The *Zacchini* case had very unusual facts—it involved a "human cannonball" act—but in terms of the development and understanding of the law, strange, unusual facts in cases often wind up producing strange outcomes, and they are harder to use in a general, analogical manner for application in other scenarios. It simply is hard to compare a new client's facts to the facts of a precedent case when the facts of the precedent case are strange, unique, and complicated.

The strange facts of the *Zacchini* case produced a slightly skewed outcome. The claimant won, but he won against the First Amendment freedom of press broadcast rights of a news station. A bona fide member of the press ultimately was punished (in the civil law sense—paying damages) for reporting the news so that Mr. Zacchini could enjoy his publicity rights. That outcome haunts the law, because normally, in the average factual scenario, a First Amendment news publication defense would defeat a

---

[4] For every LeBron James, Ginger Rogers, or Taylor Swift, there may be a Paris Hilton, Kim Kardashian, or Kevin Federline.

[5] *Zacchini v. Scripps-Howard Broadcasting Co.*, 433 U.S. 562 (1977).

right of publicity claim on most days of the week and twice on Sundays. Nevertheless, we are stuck with *Zacchini*—at least until the Supreme Court decides to adjudicate its second right of publicity case.

As announced a moment ago, the strange facts of *Zacchini* involve a human cannonball act:[6]

[6] Thumbnail-size excerpts of Photographs Depicting Hugo Zacchini, the subject of the case, *Zacchini v. Scripps-Howard Broadcasting Co.*, 433 U.S. 562 (1977).

Hugo Zacchini, Human Flying Cannonball, Faingold Studios, Cheyenne, WY

Hugo Zacchini, Hugo & Son

Hugo Zacchini, the plaintiff and petitioner, comes from a long line of human cannonballs—many Zacchinis have found a living through climbing down

the barrel of a cannon and being shot across a fairground to land in a net. One unusual aspect of the facts is the nature of the "publicity" that was protected: Zacchini spent his formative years learning and perfecting a craft that culminated in public performances that lasted all of 15 seconds. He climbed up to the mouth of the barrel of the cannon, waved a gallant greeting to the crowd, climbed down into the barrel, and was fired through the air to a waiting net. Years were spent learning how to do this and not die, but the whole act easily could be captured for airing in the "human interest" segment of the last two minutes of a nightly news broadcast. And that is exactly what happened.[7]

Scripps Howard, the respondent, was the owner of a television station in or near Cleveland, Ohio. A freelance reporter working for the station attended the county fair where Mr. Zacchini was performing. The reporter was told by Zacchini not to film the act for the news; he said he didn't want the act to be shown on the news because it was his livelihood, and he worried that if people saw it for free on television, they would have no incentive to come all the way down to the fair and pay the extra admission charge required to see his act. The news reporter was miffed, and he attended the fair the next day to surreptitiously film the act—all 15 seconds of it. The station then aired it in the "human interest" segment at the end of the late evening news broadcast. The station did try to ameliorate what Zacchini said he feared from a broadcast of his act on the news: in the

---

[7] *Id.* at 564.

segment, the news reporter told the viewers to see the show in person, stating, "Believe me, although it's not a long act, it's a thriller . . . and you really need to see it in person . . . to appreciate it. . . ."[8] But air the entire act, they did.

Zacchini sued. The case went through the Ohio state court system and on to the United States Supreme Court to determine if the Ohio publicity law and how it was applied gelled with the First Amendment freedom of press and of expression. The Supreme Court dwelled on the fact that the news station had aired Zacchini's *entire* act. This, of course, was only possible because he had such an unusual profession. But in the analysis of the court, it was unfair for a station to broadcast a man's life's work, the culmination of his achievements, all at once, and for free, in the name of news reporting.

UNJUST ENRICHMENT, JUST DESERTS, AND INCENTIVIZING TALENT FOR THE GREATER PUBLIC GOOD

In *Zacchini,* the Court explained and justified the right of publicity on three public policy grounds:

(1) **Don't take for free what everyone else pays for**. This is a classic equitable policy against what is called ***unjust enrichment***. If it would be unfair for someone to profit at your expense, you can ask the court to stop this. Everyone was supposed to pay to see Zacchini,

[8] *Id.* at 582.

not just turn on the nightly news and see him perform his entire act for free.[9]

(2) **The need to reward the sweat of the brow of entertainers and celebrities who spend years perfecting their craft.**[10] This is pretty close to the Nimmer formulation, and also mirrors the United Kingdom's justification for protecting intellectual property rights—because someone labored (laboured) to create something original and should therefore be rewarded for the labor. It also follows a "**just deserts**" theory wherein those who work hard to perfect their art or sport should get what they deserve in the protection of the persona and image they have created.

(3) **The need to encourage people to invest effort in creative endeavors that lead to fame and celebrity status, because that will enrich society as a whole.** This is the exact American public policy supporting the American recognition of intellectual property rights.[11] The United States protects the works of artists, authors, and inventors not because we want them to be directly rewarded for their labor and good works, but because we want the general public to benefit from new, creative, original works and inventions. The author or inventor is rewarded as a secondary consequence of this

---

[9] *See id.* at 576.

[10] *Id.* at 576–77.

[11] U.S. Const. art. I § 8, cl. 8 spells out that copyright and patent rights are afforded in order to benefit the public good.

> public policy. With *Zacchini*, this theory is stretched a bit (which probably explains why it is listed third, and after the "labor" and "just deserts" theories for rewarding effort) because the general public gets little more than a gasp from the spectacle of Zacchini's achievements. Yet, entertainment is a recognized public good, and Zacchini delivers entertainment.[12]

In the end, *Zacchini* is limited by its facts. Zacchini prevailed, but only because of his unique, complicated facts. The First Amendment freedom of the press still carries a high trump card that will win the trick in most encounters with the right of publicity. But the power has its limits, and one distinctly defined limit is when a news outlet captures and airs for free the entire life's achievement of a celebrity.

INTELLECTUAL PROPERTY THEORIES

Although celebrities and sports figures protected by the right of publicity do not necessarily engage in highly intellectual activities, and there is no requirement that celebrities or athletes need to create or invent something beneficial to the public, over the decades, the majority of the theoretical justifications for the protection of personality rights have come to parallel the justifications for the protection of intellectual property: (1) to encourage the development of skills and the amassing of accomplishments that coincidentally lead to valuable

---

[12] *Id.*

celebrity-status and fame so as to benefit society and culture (the intellectual property theory of the United States);[13] (2) to reward artists and entertainers for their accomplishments;[14] (3) to protect property rights earned through effort and labor, honing one's skills or perfecting one's art (the Nimmer and British/Lockean theory of property and intellectual property rights);[15] (4) to prevent unjust enrichment at the expense of others, taking for free what others pay for (a nearly universal concept of fairness and equity);[16] and (5) to compensate for a wrong inflicted on the claimant under a simple tort theory of a duty not to harm, that is breached,

---

[13] *See* Martin H. Redish & Kelsey B. Shust, *The Right of Publicity and the First Amendment in the Modern Age of Commercial Speech*, 56 WM. & MARY L. REV. 1443, 1463 (2015); *Zacchini*, 433 U.S. at 576–77; *Cardtoons, L.C. v. Major League Baseball Players Ass'n*, 95 F.3d 959, 973 (10th Cir. 1996).

[14] Redish & Shust, *supra*, at 1456; Michael Madow, *Private Ownership of Public Image: Popular Cultural and Publicity Rights*, 81 CALIF. L. REV. 125, 176 (1993); Melville Nimmer, *The Right of Publicity*, 19 LAW & CONTEMP. PROBS. 203, 223 (1954).

[15] Redish & Shust, *supra*, at 1456; Roberta Rosenthal Kwall, *Fame*, 73 IND. L.J. 1, 41 (1997); Madow, *supra*, at 176; Nimmer, *supra*, at 223. *See also* JOHN LOCKE, SECOND TREATISE OF CIVIL GOVERNMENT 25–36 (L. DeKoster ed., 1978).

[16] *See* Redish & Shust, *supra*, at 1500; Harry Kalven, Jr., *Privacy in Tort Law-Were Warren and Brandeis Wrong?*, 31 LAW & CONTEMP. PROBS. 326, 331 (1966). *See also Carson v. Here's Johnny Portable Toilets, Inc.*, 698 F.2d 831, 837 (6th Cir. 1983); *Bi-Rite Enters., Inc. v. Button Master*, 555 F. Supp. 1188, 1198 (S.D.N.Y. 1983).

causing harm (another nearly universal concept of tort law).[17]

ECONOMIC THEORIES

Economics takes the right of publicity into a more highly theoretical territory. By way of background, the four cornerstone principles of law and economics[18] are:

- Mathematical and scientific methods of analysis and demonstration;
- The characterization of legal phenomena as incentives and costs;
- The rhetorical economic concept of efficiency; and
- Rational choice theory as corrected by the modern behavioral social sciences, cognitive studies, and brain science.[19]

Using an economic analysis, the economic justifications for the right of publicity are that

---

[17] *See* Sheldon W. Halpern, *The Right of Publicity: Commercial Exploitation of the Associative Value of Personality*, 39 VAND. L. REV. 1199, 1255 (1986); *Haelan Labs.*, 202 F.2d at 866.

[18] *See* Michael D. Murray, *The Great Recession and the Rhetorical Canons of Law and Economics*, 58 LOY. L. REV. 101, 108, 116–17 (2012); Michael D. Murray, *After the Great Recession: Law and Economics' Topics of Invention and Arrangement & Tropes of Style*, 58 LOY. L. REV. 717, 721 (2012).

[19] *See* ROBERT COOTER & THOMAS ULEN, LAW & ECONOMICS 2, 3, 4, 5, 41–43 (5th ed. 2008); RICHARD A. POSNER, ECONOMIC ANALYSIS OF LAW 3–4, 9, 13, 21, 24–25, 495–96 (7th ed. 2007); Grant M. Hayden & Stephen E. Ellis, *Law and Economics After Behavioral Economics*, 55 U. KAN. L. REV. 629 (2007).

enforcement of publicity rights incentivizes celebrities and sports figures to bear the costs and invest the resources of time and energy to persevere to develop highly valuable skills and talents. If publicity rights are protected properly, talented individuals will make a rational decision to strive to get better and better in their art, craft, or sport. It is efficient for society to allocate resources to the protection of the right because celebrities and sports figures create more wealth and public benefit than the cost of protection, and the development of better sports and better entertainment has a positive effect on society's enjoyment of life well beyond the improvements in the celebrity's or athlete's quality of life.

This theory has been criticized because the counter-analysis is also rational, namely that most celebrities and sports figures are driven to perform by incentives other than the possible exploitation of endorsements and product promotions. Only a rare few will reach the level where their endorsement activities will exceed the compensation they receive for performing their art, craft, or sport. Therefore, the right of publicity works no incentivizing role in their lives.

MORAL RIGHTS THEORY

Some authors conflate the natural rights theory of publicity rights with the equitable and just deserts theories espoused by Nimmer, *Zacchini*, and others. But beyond this overlap, there is a deeper and richer theory of protection of a creative individual's personality and persona that is distinctly un-

American: moral rights. The concept of moral rights in the law originates with German Romantic philosophers, especially Immanuel Kant, and was first applied in legal contexts in France in the mid-nineteenth century. Moral rights adds a dimension to the publicity argument by tying a person's dignity and inherent humanity to their image and persona. Thus, personality becomes a right to be protected from actions of others that would disrespect and threaten the dignity of the person. There is a considerable overlap between privacy and publicity in this formulation—private persons suffer a personal harm from actions that expose the person to unwanted attention, disgrace, or indignities to their person, and more famous people suffer a different kind of personal harm from appropriation of their image and persona when these aspects of personality are then associated with persons, products, businesses, or causes of which the person does not approve and does not wish to promote or be associated with.

The United States has not warmly embraced the concept of moral rights in the art world when the threat to dignity comes from certain ways in which the works of artists are treated (destruction or mutilation of works, or failure to give attribution to the true artist being the two most common threats),[20] and similarly has not embraced the moral rights philosophy of personality in the publicity rights area, either. But it should be noted that this moral rights

---

[20] *See, e.g.*, DUBOFF, KING, & MURRAY, ART LAW IN A NUTSHELL, ch. 14 (5th ed. 2017).

of personality theory is the prevalent theory supporting the extension of rights that parallel or replicate the right of publicity when adopted and enforced in most nations that follow a civil law tradition and that recognize publicity rights.[21]

CONSUMER PROTECTION

The last justification for the recognition and enforcement of the right of publicity is one of consumer protection. This view of publicity overlaps the rationale for trademark law which is wholly centered on avoiding trade practices that may confuse consumers as to the quality, nature, source, origin, or sponsorship of goods.[22] In the publicity context, this theory manifests itself most directly in the federal Lanham Act actions of false endorsement and false designation of origin, discussed below in Chapter 8. There also are state business tort or unfair competition laws that can be used to vindicate an unauthorized appropriation of a person's name,

---

[21] *See, e.g.*, Lakshmi Kruttika Vijay and Rohan Sharma, *Celebrities: Just what are their personality rights?* (Dec. 27, 2016), https://www.vantageasia.com/celebrities-just-what-are-their-personality-rights/; International Trademark Association, *Right of Publicity*, (2017) https://www.inta.org/Advocacy/Pages/RightofPublicity.aspx. In common law countries (British-influenced countries and former colonies of the British Empire) other than the United States, the concept of a right of publicity most often is tied to the legal concept of "passing off," which largely parallels the American actions of "false endorsement" and "false designation of origin," discussed below in Chapter 8.

[22] *See* DUBOFF, KING, & MURRAY, ART LAW IN A NUTSHELL, *supra*, ch. 13.

image, or likeness when used in a commercial activity involving advertising or trade.

CHAPTER 5

REQUIREMENTS OF A RIGHT OF PUBLICITY ACTION

The basic requirements (elements) of a right of publicity claim are:

- defendant's appropriation of plaintiff's name, image, or likeness or other aspects of plaintiff's persona;
- use of these elements of personality to the defendant's advantage, commercially or otherwise;
- with lack of consent; and
- causing injury to the plaintiff.[1]

The injury must be connected to and caused by the actions of the defendant. The right of publicity allows a person to recover damages only for pecuniary gain from misappropriation of their name, image, or likeness. In contrast to the right of privacy, the right of publicity is not intended to protect the person's feelings, but provides a cause of action where a defendant has been unjustly enriched by misappropriation of the person's valuable public persona or image. If plaintiff has other injuries caused by the defendant, such as severe emotional distress, the plaintiff can allege and attempt to prove

---

[1] *E.g.*, Restatement (Third) of Unfair Competition §§ 46–49 (1995); Restatement (Second) of Torts § 652 (1977); *Hart v. Elec. Arts, Inc.*, 717 F.3d 141, 151 & n.13 (3d Cir. 2013); *Comedy III Prods., Inc. v. Gary Saderup, Inc.*, 21 P.3d 797, 801 (Cal. 2001).

other claims against the defendant, such as a traditional privacy claim, or a claim for intentional infliction of emotional distress. But a publicity claim is for publicity-type damages or injunctive relief.

IS FAME A REQUIREMENT?

The right of publicity protects a person from an unwanted and unconsented appropriation of the value of a publicly recognizable persona. In contrast to the right of privacy where plaintiffs generally are (or are attempting to be) very private persons for whom exposure to publicity activity is harmful to their dignity and mental state, the typical plaintiff in a right of publicity action is a very public person—a celebrity of some kind. The modern action is based in property, and a simple formula for trespass on a property right is that you are the owner of the property in question, and someone else is using or taking advantage of it. Some jurisdictions follow this thought to its logical conclusion and make it a requirement that the plaintiff actually have a recognizable publicity interest to protect. In these jurisdictions, plaintiffs must establish the fame or value of their names, images, and persona as a necessary element of the right of publicity cause of action.[2]

---

[2] *See, e.g.*, *Ji v. Bose Corp.*, 538 F. Supp. 2d 349, 351 (D. Mass. 2008), *aff'd*, 626 F.3d 116 (1st Cir. 2010) (plaintiff model did not establish that she had a recognizable and valuable image and likeness to protect); *Pesina v. Midway Mfg. Co.*, 948 F. Supp. 40, 42 (N.D. Ill. 1996) (plaintiff claiming the infringement of the right of publicity must show that, prior to the defendant's use, the plaintiff's name, likeness, or persona had commercial value); *Bi-*

In jurisdictions that do not impose this upfront prerequisite (which is to say the majority of jurisdictions), the relative lack of fame or publicity value possessed by a plaintiff simply will be a factor in the amount of damages the plaintiff may recover. Plaintiffs of relatively limited fame and low publicity value still can sue for injunctive relief and whatever pecuniary damages may have been suffered as a result of the unconsented appropriation of their name, image, or persona.

COMMERCIAL SPEECH RIGHT OF PUBLICITY ACTIONS

A use of a famous person's name, image, or likeness in the context of commercial speech (i.e., advertising of a product or service) is the paradigmatic scenario for a right of publicity claim. In the commercial speech context, all of the elements of the claim are aligned:

- The advertiser appropriated the plaintiff's image or persona *because* it is valuable—*because* it will attract consumers to the advertiser's product or service;
- The advertiser made money either in increased sales or saved money from not having to pay for the sponsorship or endorsement;

Rite Enterprises, Inc. v. Button Master, 555 F. Supp. 1188, 1198–99 (S.D.N.Y.), *supplemented sub nom. Bi-Rite v. Button Master*, 578 F. Supp. 59 (S.D.N.Y. 1983) (same).

- The plaintiff lost money—she was not paid for the sponsorship or for a percentage of sales, or was insulted by the unconsented association with the advertiser's products or services;
- Other public policies are all in alignment—consumer confusion from the false suggestion of endorsement; unjust enrichment of the advertiser at the plaintiff's expense; denial of just deserts from labor well spent—all of these policies support recovery in the commercial speech situation.

The commercial speech context also lessens the pressures against recovery brought about by the First Amendment freedoms of press and expression (discussed here and in Chapter 9, *infra*). Commercial speech is the lowest form of *protected* speech in the First Amendment cosmos. (Anything lower is *unprotected* speech that is highly regulated or outright banned—obscenity, fighting words, defamation, true threats, and child pornography). Under First Amendment jurisprudence, commercial speech is all about business, so it rarely edifies or educates the audience or enriches the listeners. It may be entertaining for a few seconds, but always in the context of a crass pitch for sales. Therefore, many of the most memorable (and successful) right of publicity claims have occurred in the commercial speech context:

Celebrity	Image[3]	What was protected
Bette Midler (singer, performer)		The sound of Midler's singing voice mimicked by one of her backup singers from the "Harlettes," in an ad for a Ford automobile. —*Midler v. Ford Motor Co.*, 849 F.2d 460 (9th Cir. 1988)
Don Newcombe (pitcher for MLB Dodgers)		His high kick windup on the pitcher's mound and his slightly altered jersey number (36 changed to 39) used in an advertisement for Killian's Irish Red beer. —*Newcombe v. Adolf Coors Co.*, 157 F.3d 686 (9th Cir. 1998)

[3] Thumbnail-size images of the plaintiffs in landmark right of publicity cases cited in the table: Bette Midler and the Harlettes, Don Newcombe, Don Henley, Kareem Abdul Jabbar, Tony Twist, and Tom Waits.

Celebrity	Image[3]	What was protected
Don Henley (singer for the *Eagles*)		His name used in the advertising for henley shirts. —*Henley v. Dillard Dep't Stores*, 46 F. Supp. 2d 587 (N.D. Tex. 1999)
Kareem Abdul-Jabbar (college and professional basketball player)		His appearance playing college basketball (under the name Lew Alcindor) used in an advertisement for Oldsmobile cars. —*Abdul-Jabbar v. General Motors Corp.*, 85 F.3d 407 (9th Cir. 1996)
Tony Twist (hockey player)		His name and reputation as an "enforcer" used with a comic book character, and in certain promotional and subscription pages for the comic, *Spawn*. —*Doe v. TCI Cablevision*, 110

Celebrity	Image[3]	What was protected
		S.W.3d 363 (Mo. 2003)
Tom Waits (singer, performer)		The raspy dry sound of Waits' singing voice mimicked in an ad for Doritos. —*Waits v. Frito-Lay, Inc.*, 978 F.2d 1093 (9th Cir. 1992)

Commercial speech is an ideal climate for a right of publicity action even if it arises from the mere mention of an aspect of a celebrity's persona. It is not necessary for the celebrity's entire name, image, or likeness to be appropriated, as long as the defendant conjures up the valuable persona through its advertising.

Carson v. Here's Johnny Portable Toilets[4] is one such case of "appropriation of things associated with a celebrity" where the plaintiff, Johnny Carson, the former and long-time host of NBC's the Tonight Show, brought suit against an outdoor toilet supply company that helpfully went by the name that caused the lawsuit in the first place: "Here's Johnny Portable Toilets," with the byline: "World's Foremost Commodian." The obvious play on the words "commode" and "comedian" did not make Carson laugh. Instead, he sued.

The basis for the assertion of publicity rights was that Carson was intimately connected to the phrase "Here's Johnny" because in the opening of every Tonight Show broadcast, Carson's sidekick, Ed McMahon, announced Carson with the phrase, "Heea-eeeeeers Johnny." As noted earlier in Chapter

[4] *Carson v. Here's Johnny Portable Toilets, Inc.*, 698 F.2d 831 (6th Cir. 1983).

1, the invocation of a tagline as a stand-in for the entire persona of a celebrity reflects a rather broad interpretation of publicity rights. Nevertheless, Carson prevailed.

The case of *Lohan v. E-Trade* (Cal. Super. Ct. 2011),[5] features Lindsay Lohan, a formerly successful child and teenage film star, who did not like what she saw on a certain Super Bowl Sunday. What she saw was a clever E-Trade stock trading site advertisement[6] that featured the popular character of "stock-trading baby" and a surprise guest—another toddler named

[5] *Lohan v. E*Trade Sec. LLC*, No. MOTION M-5262X, 2010 N.Y. Slip Op. 87873(U), 2010 WL 4608641 (N.Y. App. Div. Nov. 16, 2010); Jennifer Peltz, *Lindsay Lohan ends lawsuit over E-Trade baby ad*, USA TODAY (Sep. 21, 2010, 8:48 AM), http://usatoday30.usatoday.com/life/people/2010-09-21-lohan-settles-etrade-suit_N.htm.

[6] Thumbnail-size excerpt of a frame from the E*Trade "Milkaholic Lindsay" commercial, at issue in the case, *Lohan v. E*Trade Sec. LLC*, No. MOTION M-5262X, 2010 WL 4608641 (N.Y. App. Div. Nov. 16, 2010).

Lindsay. The male toddler is shown having a video conference with yet another female toddler, who asks him why he didn't call her the past evening. After some explanation, the female asks, "And that milkaholic Lindsay wasn't over?" in an accusatory tone. To which the male toddler stutters, ". . . Lindsay?" And into the video frame stumbles "Lindsay," a red-headed female toddler, who delivers the punch line: "Milk-a-what??" (you probably should Google this one—"Lindsay Lohan E-Trade Baby Commercial"—so as to see the actual video in question. Perhaps the video will still be at http://www.youtube.com/watch?v=5QS9rIZcjaw by the time you look for it).

Lindsay Lohan's claim is a bit "complicated"—which many people would describe as "wrong-headed." You see, at this time of the commercial's airing, Lohan's adult career in film had fallen on rough times, and the former child and teen star had had a run of trouble with alcohol and drugs. The once perky film star was not looking so cute and perky anymore. Lohan perceived that E-Trade was capitalizing on her alcohol problems. The alleged link in the advertisement was that any mention of the first name, "Lindsay," in proximity to a term that sounded like "alcoholic," would immediately call to mind the young actress Lindsay Lohan and her well-publicized drinking problems. The E-Trade people cast a toddler with reddish-colored hair in the role of "Lindsay," too. And since the use occurred during the most valuable advertising event of the year, the Super Bowl broadcast, the actress believed that, no matter how much she herself had dragged her own name through the mud, E-Trade was trying to gain an advantage by the association of its name and good sense of humor with that of the drinky actress.

Many commentators reacted with something equivalent to, "Lindsay, get over yourself!" They charged that Lohan had certainly not achieved the "one name" status of certain other actors and musicians—"Beyoncé," "Cher," "Prince," "Madonna," "Bono," "Arnold" (pronounced "Ah-noald" to match the thick Austrian accent of the beloved actor and former Republican governor of California), to name a few. This select group did not include "Lindsay" for Lindsay Lohan. Nevertheless, Lohan pursued a legal claim asserting a publicity violation against E-Trade. The end of the story?—The two settled for an undisclosed amount.[7] Lohan was apparently "satisfied" with the amount, and the two otherwise went their separate ways.

The above cases show the risk of using any celebrity's name, image, or likeness in a commercial advertising or promotional sense without getting authorization and without paying for the value of the image. But not every commercial speech use of a celebrity's name or image triggers the test. A court considered the use of Beyoncé Knowles-Carter's name, "BEYONCÉ" (which is a trademark owned by the performer), by a company that specializes in the "about to be" and "recently engaged" population by running and

[7] *See* Peltz, *supra*; Carlin Miller, *Lindsay Lohan E-Trade "Milkaholic" Lawsuit Settled*, CBS News (Sep. 22, 2010, 11:31 AM), https://www.cbsnews.com/news/lindsay-lohan-e-trade-milkaholic-lawsuit-settled/.

advertising their business under the name, "FEYONCÉ," intending the pronunciation to be roughly the same as "fiancé." Ms. Knowles-Carter sought to protect her rights through the federal and state trademark law enforcement mechanisms of trademark infringement, false designation of origin, and trademark dilution, supported by claims regarding deceptive business practices and unfair competition. Although Ms. Knowles-Carter is at the top of the A-List of celebrities, the court did not believe it was sufficiently likely that she would suffer any publicity damage (in the form of trademark infringement, false designation, or dilution harms) by the sound-alike name differing from her own name by only one letter, and so it denied Ms. Knowles-Carter's motion for summary judgment in the case. *Knowles-Carter v. Feyonce, Inc.*, 347 F. Supp. 3d 217 (S.D.N.Y. 2018).

COMMERCIAL VS. NONCOMMERCIAL USAGE

Although all people have the right to be free from the unauthorized exploitation of their likeness, not every publication of someone's likeness gives rise to an appropriation action. Most right of publicity statutes and common law rules require the use of the plaintiff's name, image, or likeness to be in the course of a commercial activity. Commercial speech (advertising) is a sure-fire use in commerce and trade, as discussed in the prior section, but not every other use even in a for-profit venture will be characterized as "commercial." This is especially true if the for-profit activity has First Amendment expression involved in it.

In *Downing v. Abercrombie & Fitch,*[8] the defendant retail clothing store used photographs of Downing, a famous surfer, in defendant's clothing catalog. This use was held to violate the surfer's right of publicity because the catalog constituted a commercial advertising of products, and it did not convey news, commentary on surfing, or other public interest information beyond the appropriated images of surfers.[9]

George Downing, the first surfer on the left

---

[8] *Downing v. Abercrombie & Fitch*, 265 F.3d 994, 1004 (9th Cir. 2001).

[9] *See also Toney v. L'Oreal USA, Inc.*, 406 F.3d 905, 908 (7th Cir. 2005) (unauthorized use of model's photo on packaging of hair product was a use to help sell the product, not a news or public information use); *Christoff v. Nestle USA, Inc.*, 213 P.3d 132, 136 (Cal. 2009) (unauthorized use of image on coffee label was a use to help sell the product).

In contrast, in *Dora v. Frontline Video*,[10] the makers of a documentary, *The Legends of Malibu*, used images of Mickey (or "Miki") Dora (at right in the image below), another famous surfer, in a documentary that commented on surfers and their surfing lifestyle. The documentary was not commercial advertising for products or services (i.e., not commercial speech), and instead was found to be pure speech with archival, educational, and commentary value on a newsworthy public interest topic.[11]

Mickey Dora (at right) surfing in Malibu[12]

[10] *Dora v. Frontline Video, Inc.*, 18 Cal. Rptr. 2d 790, 792 (Ct. App. 1993).

[11] *See also Tyne v. Time Warner Entm't Co.*, 901 So. 2d 802 (Fla. 2005) (the term "commercial purpose" as used in Fla. Rt. of Publicity statute does not apply to publications, including motion pictures, which do not directly promote a product or service); *Nichols v. Moore*, 396 F. Supp. 2d 783, 787 (E.D. Mich. 2005), *aff'd*, 477 F.3d 396 (6th Cir. 2007) (same).

[12] Image of Mickey Dora surfing, the subject of *Dora v. Frontline Video, Inc.*, 18 Cal. Rptr. 2d 790, 792 (Ct. App. 1993).

The use of a celebrity's image in connection with the attempt to report news still must be fair and not misleading. In *Solano v. Playgirl, Inc.*,[13] *Playgirl* used on the cover of their magazine plaintiff Solano's image taken from Solano's appearance on the *Baywatch* television show. Although *Playgirl* sometimes publishes news and commentary, and always publishes matters of great interest to a certain segment of the public, in this case Solano was raising a publicity claim of false advertising that cast him in a false light.

The cover photo and its surrounding text headings had made it appear that Solano was to be one of the "TV Guys," "Primetime's Sexy Young Stars Exposed," or "Sizzling Centerfolds" who were exposed in the

---

[13] *Solano v. Playgirl, Inc.*, 292 F.3d 1078, 1082 (9th Cir. 2002).

nude in the magazine. However, only one small photograph of Solano appeared inside the magazine, in which he was fully dressed, along with a short biography of the plaintiff emphasizing his performance on *Baywatch*. The use was held to be actionable and not related to a newsworthy event or matter of public interest because *Playgirl* suggested that nude photographs of plaintiff would be found in the issue when they were not. Solano's picture was chosen as the cover image to help sell the magazine (hence the commercial use hook), when in fact he had not agreed to pose for or even be interviewed by the magazine.

The court in the *Toffoloni v. LFP Publ'g Grp.* (aka, Hustler Magazine) case[14] followed a similar logic in denying the newsworthiness defense of Hustler Magazine regarding the printing of twenty-year-old nude images of wrestler Nancy Benoit a short time after Benoit had been murdered by her husband, fellow wrestler Chris Benoit. The images had absolutely no connection to her murder case, and the court ruled that they did not fall within the newsworthiness exception and were not published incident to any matter of public interest.

PUBLIC FIGURES AND FIRST AMENDMENT FREEDOMS

Celebrities bring the most publicity actions, which makes complete sense, because the most popular celebrities are the most likely targets of exploitation

---

[14] *Toffoloni v. LFP Publ'g Grp., LLC,* 572 F.3d 1201, 1213 (11th Cir. 2009).

and appropriation. For lesser luminaries or complete non-celebrities, the lawsuits are expensive and time-consuming, and non-celebrities most likely will not invest the time and money required to vindicate an unconsented use of their name, image, or likeness.[15]

Celebrities also seek out or at least anticipate publicity in their lives in the same way that politicians and prominent business people do. Which means that most often right of publicity plaintiffs will be designated as public figures under the First Amendment. The consequences of this designation are that when a public figure brings a right of publicity claim in a non-commercial speech context (i.e., when the case does not involve advertising of a product or service), the public figure often will have an uneasy time because of the freedom of press and freedom of expression clauses of the First Amendment. The speech of the defendant will not be relegated to the lowest tier of protected speech because it is not commercial speech.

The law handles public figures differently from private persons who do not seek out nor expect publicity from the media. Public figures must expect news coverage of their actions, and when a public figure's adversaries in a right of publicity suit are the news media, newspapers, and other media outlets, these news entities have a First Amendment freedom

---

[15] Of course, there are those who will sue on principle, even if the principal of the equation is questionable. *See, e.g., Murray v. New York Magazine Co.*, 267 N.E.2d 256, 258 (N.Y. 1971) (man photographed for cover of defendant magazine sued under the New York Civil Rights Law § 51 because he didn't want to be portrayed as an Irish immigrant).

of press to publish information and images of newsworthy people and events. Even outside of the purely news reporting context, social or artistic commentary can constitute a protected artistic form of expression sufficient to defeat a publicity claim.

In *Hoffman v. Capital Cities/ABC, Inc.*,[16] Dustin Hoffman brought suit against the owners of Los Angeles Magazine for publishing an altered photograph of Hoffman in the March 1997 "Fabulous Hollywood Issue!," in a section entitled "The Ultimate Fashion Show." This magazine section featured altered photographs of several iconic stars in iconic roles (e.g., Cary Grant being menaced by a plane in *North by Northwest*), culminating in the photograph of Hoffman in his role as the cross-dressing *Tootsie*, but instead of his red sequined gown from the 1982 movie, Hoffman's appearance

---

[16] *See, e.g., Hoffman v. Capital Cities/ABC, Inc.*, 255 F.3d 1180 (9th Cir. 2001).

was digitally-altered to wear current fashions. As described in the article: "Dustin Hoffman isn't a drag in a butter-colored silk gown by Richard Tyler and Ralph Lauren heels."

Hoffman initially prevailed at the trial court for this unauthorized and uncompensated appropriation of his portrait and name, but the case was reversed at the United States Court of Appeals for the Ninth Circuit because the court found that the magazine had included the altered photograph in an article commenting on the upcoming season's fashions, and not in an advertisement (i.e., not commercial speech) for the clothing. This finding was made even though the magazine provided information on where the clothing could be purchased, and there was little commentary in the article other than the altered photographs showing highly fashionable clothing.

Neither was Dustin Hoffman known to be a fashion symbol in men's or women's clothing, so the use of his image in this article on fashion was somewhat randomly chosen. But fashion is a matter of great public interest, and the First Amendment commentary carried the day in defeating Hoffman's publicity claim.

ARTISTIC COMMENTARY ON SPORTS HISTORY

When Tiger Woods won the 1997 Masters Golf Tournament, his first major tournament victory as a professional golfer, he was the youngest golfer ever to win the Masters (age 21), he won it with the largest margin of victory ever in the Masters (12 strokes under his closest opponent), he was the first person of African American ancestry to win the tournament, and the first of Asian American ancestry (owing to his father being African American and his mother being Asian American). In short, a lot of history was made at that golf tournament. Tiger also became established as a public figure around which a great deal of public interest is focused. This made him newsworthy and a subject of public affairs attention and commentary. Rick Rush, a sports artist, wanted to celebrate and commemorate the history that Tiger Woods made in Augusta during that tournament (and make a little money in the process).

Rush created a painting[17] that was serialized into an issue of limited edition serigraphs. By "limited," it means he only made five thousand of them. The images showed Tiger Woods three times in various poses from the tournament. It also showed Tiger's caddie, his opponent's caddie, the Butler Cabin of the Augusta National Golf Club where the Masters Tournament is held, and depicted some ghostly images of earlier Masters champions that appear in the sky above the cabin (in the firmament over the tournament, as it were) positioned in front of a

[17] Reduced-size excerpt of Rick Rush, *The Masters of Augusta*, the painting at issue in *ETW Corp. v. Jireh Pub., Inc.*, 332 F.3d 915 (6th Cir. 2003).

ghostly image of the famous leader board at August National.

In the case, *ETW Corp. v. Jireh Pub.*,[18] Tiger Woods sued Rick Rush—or, as the title of the case indicates, Tiger's corporation, ETW Inc., sued Rick Rush's printer, Jireh Publications. Tiger asserted a trademark claim of false endorsement. The gist of this federal claim was that the use of an image of Tiger Woods in this context suggests Tiger Woods' endorsement of the product (the art print) and of the artist, Rick Rush. This is the type of "publicity" claim that is enforced by a federal Lanham Act claim under a theory of consumer protection from confusion—the confusion being over whether Tiger endorsed the art print or Rick Rush. To be sure, Tiger's endorsement means something; as noted in Chapter 1, Tiger Woods often made a great deal more in endorsements than he ever did actually playing golf.[19] The claim seeks to vindicate the denial of the normal quid pro quo arrangement: if you want Tiger's endorsement, you pay for it—everyone else pays for it—and if you use the image without paying for it you are unjustly enriched, and consumers might be confused.

Tiger also brought a state law claim under Ohio's right of publicity law, the same law that was at issue in *Zacchini*. This was a more standard publicity

[18] *ETW Corp. v. Jireh Pub., Inc.*, 332 F.3d 915 (6th Cir. 2003).

[19] Jesse Oxfeld, *Tiger Woods Earns 83 Times More Money Endorsing Things Than Playing Golf Plus other athletes' income stats*, Adweek (Jun. 30, 2015, 1:55pm EDT), http://www.adweek.com/news/advertising-branding/tiger-woods-earns-83-times-more-money-endorsing-things-playing-golf-165649.

action: use of Tiger's image, in a commercial venture (to sell art prints), without his consent, and causing alleged publicity damage to Tiger. The damage amounts to lost revenue rather than any mental state damages for one such as Tiger who was constantly in the public eye; but everyone has to pay for the use of Tiger's image and likeness, and Rick Rush didn't.

Both claims came down to the question of fair use, and fair use in false endorsement and right of publicity claims generally means: "Whether and how the First Amendment limits or precludes the claims of the celebrity when the defendant has used the image or likeness of the celebrity for expressive (speech) purposes." Sports and athletics, like clothing and fashions, are matters of great public interest in this country, and Tiger Woods' victory had greater societal implications regarding the achievements of traditionally underrepresented minorities in sports such as golf. As in the *Hoffman* case, in *ETW*, the commentary on current events and public affairs represented by Rick Rush's artistic expression of a newsworthy, historical event defeated Tiger Woods' demand for payment for his unauthorized and uncompensated endorsement.

STATISTICS, FACTS, AND PUBLIC INTEREST INFORMATION

The publication of statistics and facts of matters that are within the general public interest, including facts and statistics of sports figures and celebrities, is not subject to protection under the right of publicity. This has been litigated several times, and each time the cases have resulted in a ruling that the publication of information concerning sports figures' names, statistics, and records of achievements is not actionable under the right of publicity.

In *Gionfriddo v. Major League Baseball*,[20] the court considered the use of players' names, statistics, and images in videos commemorating All-Star baseball games and World Series events. The court held that the reporting of baseball statistics along with the names and images of the players who created the statistics was protected reporting of newsworthy information, and a matter of great public interest, which were strong First Amendment reasons to deny a right of publicity claim regarding the publication.

Similarly, in *C.B.C. Distribution & Mktg., Inc. v. Major League Baseball Advanced Media*,[21] the court evaluated the publication of lists, thumbnail images, and statistics about baseball players for use in running a for-profit fantasy baseball information service. The court again held that the underlying information has First Amendment current affairs value that preempts players' right of publicity in their identity. Even though the publication was used in a money-making venture, it was not used in commercial advertising.

In 2018, the rationale of the holdings and outcomes of *Gionfriddo* and *CBC* was extended to collegiate

---

[20] *Gionfriddo v. Major League Baseball*, 114 Cal. Rptr. 2d 307, 310 (Ct. App. 2001).

[21] *C.B.C. Distribution & Mktg., Inc. v. Major League Baseball Advanced Media, L.P.*, 505 F.3d 818, 820 (8th Cir. 2007).

athletes in the case, *Daniels v. FanDuel, Inc. and DraftKings, Inc.*,[22] which held that the First Amendment "newsworthiness" protection forecloses an action by collegiate players' to prevent the use of their names, likenesses, and playing statistics in a for-profit fantasy-league gaming enterprise.

---

[22] *Daniels v. FanDuel, Inc.*, 109 N.E.3d 390, 397 (Ind. 2018) (answering certified question re: newsworthiness exception); 909 F.3d 876, 878 (7th Cir. 2018) (affirming dismissal of suit).

CHAPTER 6

POST-MORTEM RIGHT OF PUBLICITY

The post-mortem celebrity market is thriving, and some recently and not so recently deceased stars are making tens or even hundreds of millions of dollars after shuffling off the mortal coil. According to Forbes magazine in 2021, the highest paid deceased celebrities were: Roald Dahl at #1 ($513 million; bolstered by a reported $684 million paid to his estate by Netflix for Dahl's literary properties, including *Charlie and the Chocolate Factory*); the recording artists Prince ($120 million) and Michael Jackson ($75 million) were second and third respectively; Charles Schulz, of Peanuts and Charlie Brown comic fame, was #4 ($40 million); and Dr. Seuss (Theodor Geisel), creator of the *Cat in the Hat*, *Grinch*, and *Lorax*, came in at #5 ($35 million).[1] By comparison, in 2017, Michael Jackson, a perennial contender for the top spots among the deceased, led the Forbes 2017 list with $75 million from Oct. 2016–Oct. 2017, but in Oct. 2015–Oct. 2016, he made a whopping $825 million—the highest annual total for any entertainer dead or alive—largely boosted from the sale of his half of the Sony/ATV music publishing catalog.[2] The

---

[1] Abigail Freeman, *The Highest-Paid Dead Celebrities 2021*, Forbes.com (Oct. 30, 2021), https://www.forbes.com/sites/abigailfreeman/2021/10/30/the-highest-paid-dead-celebrities-2021/?sh=4af7f233839e.

[2] Zack O'Malley Greenburg, *The Top-Earning Dead Celebrities of 2017*, Forbes.com (Oct. 30, 2017), https://www.forbes.com/sites/zackomalleygreenburg/2017/10/30/the-top-earning-dead-celebrities-of-2017.

rest of the 2017 list included, in order: Arnold Palmer, golfing legend, then recently deceased ($40 million); Charles Schulz, again ($38 million); Elvis Presley, the King of Rock and Roll, still rocking the money charts after his death 40 years ago ($35 million); Bob Marley, Reggae legend ($23 million); Tom Petty, the rock and roll singer, who died in Oct. 2017 ($20 million); Prince, again ($18 million); Dr. Seuss (Theodor Geisel), again ($16 million); John Lennon, former Beatle, still "Imagining" a lot of income ($12 million); and Albert Einstein, the physicist, oldest entry on the list having died in 1955 ($10 million). Just missing the top-ten list that year was David Bowie, deceased in 2016 ($9.5 million); Elizabeth Taylor, actress, whose perfume line still sells well ($8 million); and Bettie Page, Queen of Pin-up models—from the 1950's!—and still a force in the clothing and naughty lingerie market ($7.5 million).[3] Perennial deceased standouts Marilyn Monroe, James Dean, Steve McQueen, and Jerry Garcia (very grateful in death), also did not make the 2017 top-ten list, but have often made the list in the past.

Death is normally not a bar to successful exploitation of publicity rights, as long as your estate is not domiciled in Alaska, North Dakota, Rhode Island, Wisconsin, or Wyoming when you die, which are the states that expressly do not recognize a post-mortem right of publicity, or never have recognized privacy or publicity rights for anyone, living or deceased.[4] Until

[3] *Id.*

[4] *See* the Appendix. Rhode Island and Wisconsin expressly reject post-mortem rights in their laws. Alaska, North Dakota, and

2020, New York also did not recognize the claims of the deceased. The New York rule stemmed from the origin of the right in New York State as a right of privacy; privacy being a very personal thing, it cannot be assigned or devised to one's heirs. It was viewed as a right to exploit or defend while one was living. But the legislature eventually saw the need in 2020 to the change New York's hundred and seventeen year old law to add coverage for posthumous claims of celebrities, who are defined in the law as either a " 'deceased performer' [which] means a deceased natural person domiciled in this state at the time of death who, for gain or livelihood, was regularly engaged in acting, singing, dancing, or playing a musical instrument," or a " 'deceased personality' [which] means any deceased natural person domiciled in this state at the time of death whose name, voice, signature, photograph, or likeness has commercial value at the time of his or her death, or because of his or her death, whether or not during the lifetime of that natural person the person used his or her name, voice, signature, photograph, or likeness on or in products, merchandise, or goods, or for purposes of advertising or selling, or solicitation of purchase of, products, merchandise, goods, or services." N.Y. Civ. Rights Law § 50–f(1)(a), (b) (McKinney, effective May 29, 2021). One threat that obviously was not present in 1903 was the ability to exploit deceased celebrities through digital recreations or "deepfakes," and the new law singles out treatment in "digital replicas" as

---

Wyoming have never recognized any form of a publicity or privacy "appropriation" action for living or deceased celebrities.

one of the activities prohibited in the statute. *Id.* § 50–f(1)(c).

Twenty-five states currently recognize a post-mortem right either by statute or common law.[5] Eighteen states recognize the postmortem right by statute, and the term of protection varies from ten years (Tennessee, but it can be extended indefinitely if commercial use continues after tenth year); twenty years (Virginia); thirty years (Pennsylvania); forty years (Florida, New York); fifty years (Arkansas, Illinois, Kentucky, Nevada, Texas); fifty-five years (Alabama); sixty years (Ohio); seventy years (California, Hawaii, South Dakota); seventy-five years (Washington, if the rights had value at the time of death); or one hundred years (Indiana, Oklahoma).[6]

For the seven states with common law recognition of the post-mortem right of publicity, the term is not certain (Arizona, Georgia, Michigan, Nebraska,[7] New Jersey, South Carolina, and Utah).[8]

---

[5] *See* the Appendix for the breakdown, state by state. *See also* Jennifer E. Rothman, *Rothman's Roadmap to the Right of Publicity* (2015), https://www.rightofpublicityroadmap.com/; Erik W. Kahn, Pou-I Lee, *"Delebs" and Postmortem Right of Publicity*, Landslide, vol. 8 No. 3 (Feb. 2016), https://www.americanbar.org/publications/landslide/2015-16/january-february/delebs_and_postmortem_right_publicity.html.

[6] *See* 2 J. THOMAS MCCARTHY, RIGHTS OF PUBLICITY AND PRIVACY §§ 9:30–9:44 (2d ed. 2017).

[7] Nebraska has a statutory right of publicity (phrased as privacy) provision that survives death, but it provides no term of years for the right. Neb. Rev. Stat. §§ 20–202, 20–208 (2017).

[8] Utah's statute on abuse of personal identity, Utah Code Ann. § 45–3–1 et seq., has no term of years and no indication whether it

The remaining nineteen states (including the District of Columbia) that have recognized common law publicity or privacy rights have not spoken to the issue as to whether they will be enforced posthumously, so the post-mortem right and its possible duration are not certain (Colorado, Connecticut, Delaware, District of Columbia, Idaho, Iowa, Kansas, Maine, Maryland, Minnesota, Mississippi, Missouri, Montana, New Hampshire, New Mexico, North Carolina, Oregon, Vermont, and West Virginia).[9]

Massachusetts has a publicity statute that applies to "any person,"[10] but there is no definition in the statute or interpretation in case law as to whether that means living persons only, or deceased persons, too. The Massachusetts courts have decided that the provision applies to corporate entities,[11] so the concept of a "person" is somewhat expansive in the Bay State.

The federal trademark claim of false endorsement has been held to be enforceable post-mortem.[12] This

---

applies posthumously. Louisiana's statute is limited to posthumous claims related to soldiers, and it has no specified terms of years. *See* La. Rev. Stat. § 14:102.21.

[9] *See* McCarthy, *supra;* Rothman, *supra*. *See also* the Appendix, *infra*.

[10] Mass. Gen. Laws ch. 214, § 3A.

[11] *Kam IV, Inc. v. D'Onfro*, No. 16-CV-12079-ADB, 2017 WL 3083166, at *1 n.1 (D. Mass. July 19, 2017).

[12] *See Fifty-Six Hope Rd. Music, Ltd. v. A.V.E.L.A., Inc.*, 778 F.3d 1059, 1072 (9th Cir.), *cert. denied*, 577 U.S. 957 (2015) (regarding false endorsement claim involving Bob Marley, the deceased reggae master).

federal claim parallels and sometimes overlaps the rights protected in a right of publicity action. (*See* Chapter 8).

Under the majority of states' laws, the heirs and owners of the rights of exploitation can enjoy the fruits of publicity after death if the celebrity's death occurred after the passage of the right of publicity statute. Therefore, for a celebrity who has recently passed this world, enforcement of publicity rights are guaranteed (outside of Alaska, North Dakota, Rhode Island, Wisconsin, or Wyoming). But certain courts may require that the publicity rights were granted or created by statute or common law, or at least were recognized by a court or legislature of the applicable jurisdiction, while the celebrity was alive. Under this interpretation, if the rights existed when the celebrity was alive, then the rights can be devised to the celebrity's heirs upon the celebrity's death. However, celebrities who died several decades ago, before several of the longest-term post-mortem right of publicity statutes were passed (two important examples being California and Indiana), may face problems.

The heirs of Marilyn Monroe learned this the hard way in *Shaw Family Archives Ltd. v. CMG Worldwide, Inc.*[13] At the time of her death in 1962, Marilyn Monroe had no descendible postmortem publicity rights under the laws of either New York or California, her only possible domiciles at the time of her death, and thus, the court found she lacked

[13] *Shaw Family Archives Ltd. v. CMG Worldwide, Inc.*, 486 F. Supp. 2d 309 (S.D.N.Y. 2007).

testamentary capacity to devise such rights, despite the claim that her will should have been construed as devising postmortem publicity rights that were later conferred on her by an Indiana or California statute. The court declared that only property she actually owned at the time of her death could be devised by will.[14] A similar action, *Milton Greene Archives v. Marilyn Monroe LLC*,[15] in the Ninth Circuit United States Court of Appeals came to the same conclusion in 2012—that Marilyn Monroe had no rights under New York or California law at the time she died, so she could not pass them on through her estate after death even though the rights later were "created" under California and Indiana law.[16]

---

[14] *Id.* at 314.

[15] *Milton H. Greene Archives, Inc. v. Marilyn Monroe LLC*, 692 F.3d 983 (9th Cir. 2012).

[16] *Id.* at 1000.

CHAPTER 7

COPYRIGHT PREEMPTION AND THE EFFECT OF LICENSING

The right of publicity protects different rights than copyright. Copyright exerts control over the duplication and exploitation of expressive works. The requirements of copyright protection are that an original work that is not a copy of another work (originality requirement) has been conceived of in the mind of an author (creativity requirement) and rendered into a fixed and tangible medium (fixation requirement) that can be perceived by at least one of the senses (expression requirement).[1] Copyright allows the owner of the copyright to duplicate the work or authorize the creation of duplicates or works that are derivatives of the copyrighted work (for example, a motion picture that is a derivative of a novel).

The right of publicity protects actors', athletes', and celebrities' names, likenesses, appearance, and other aspects of their persona—for example, Johnny Carson's tag line of "Here's Johnny," and the particular sound of Bette Midler's and Tom Waits' singing voices. At times, the two rights, copyright and publicity, can conflict when a copyrighted work featuring the performance of a celebrity is licensed for a particular duplication, publication, or derivative use, and the publicity rights of the actors, athletes, or celebrities appearing in that copyrighted work are

---

[1] *See* DUBOFF, KING, & MURRAY, ART LAW IN A NUTSHELL, ch. 12.

not similarly licensed, and the actors, athletes, or celebrities are not compensated for the second use of their images and personae.

If the rights asserted by a celebrity are the same rights that were licensed under copyright law to a media company or other publisher, the copyright license trumps the right of publicity claim.[2] The theory is that the exercise of the copyrights over the items protected by copyright (works fixed in a tangible medium of expression) is sufficient to preclude any publicity rights of performers whose performances also are fixed within that work.[3] Implicitly, by agreeing to allow one's voice, appearance, or performance to be fixed within a work that will protected by copyright, the performer has consented to the licensing and further use of that fixed recording under the exercise of the copyrights to the recording.

If publicity rights duplicate the rights that are covered by copyright law—such as the situation of a rebroadcast or republication of a taped event, sports contest, or publication—then copyright law might preempt the publicity claim.[4] Preemption means that

---

[2] *Laws v. Sony Music Entm't, Inc.*, 448 F.3d 1134, 1143–44 (9th Cir. 2006) (exercise of rights to copyrighted sound recording cannot violate publicity rights of singer whose voice is heard in that very recording); *Fleet v. CBS, Inc.*, 58 Cal. Rptr. 2d 645 (Ct. App. 1996) (copyrights to video recording preempt publicity claim of actor appearing in the recording).

[3] *Laws*, 448 F.3d at 1141–44; *Fleet*, 58 Cal. Rptr. 2d at 645.

[4] 17 U.S.C. § 301; *see, e.g.*, *Baltimore Orioles, Inc. v. Major League Baseball Players Ass'n*, 805 F.2d 663, 674–79 (7th Cir. 1986).

the rights asserted under a right of publicity claim are the same in every way to the rights protected under copyright law, and potentially controlled by a copyright license,[5] and so copyright law is given priority to control how the publicity rights are recognized and enforced. Right of publicity claims are not preempted if the claims attempt to adjudicate rights that are different from those covered by copyright.

Note well that in the scenario here, the actors, athletes, or celebrities are not the copyright holders of the work in question, which is typical of actors' performances in motion pictures[6] or an athletes' performance in a sporting event recorded through a copyrighted broadcast and simultaneous recording of the sporting event.[7] In the case of broadcasts of sporting events, the broadcaster and its sport league license partner (e.g., Major League Baseball, or the National Football League) would own the copyright

---

5 *Jules Jordan Video, Inc. v. 144942 Canada Inc.*, 617 F.3d 1146, 1153–54 (9th Cir. 2010); *Laws*, 448 F.3d at 1141–44.

6 Contributors to a motion picture, including the actors, director, cinematographer, and all others contributing their talents to the project, are bound by the "work made for hire" rules, 17 U.S.C. § 101 (definition of "Work made for hire"), that grant copyright ownership to the employer in control of the production, generally meaning the producers of the film. An actor's performance in a copyrighted film is controlled by the copyright owner, and it does not give rise to separate copyright or right of publicity rights that pertain to the parts of the film that feature the actor's performance in the film. *See Jules Jordan Video,* 617 F.3d at 1153–54.

7 *See Maloney v. T3Media, Inc.*, 853 F.3d 1004, 1011 (9th Cir. 2017); *Dryer v. Nat'l Football League*, 814 F.3d 938, 943 (8th Cir. 2016).

to the broadcast and simultaneous recording of the sporting event; the athletes on the field would not.

With musical recordings, the recording artists might own one part of the copyright if they are the composer or arranger of the music, another if they produce and pay for the audio recording of the music, and a third if they produce and pay for the creation of a music video. But in each instance, it may be the record company or media conglomerate that owns the various copyrights to the audio and video recordings. An indicative case of preemption in the recording industry involved the rapper "50 Cent" (known in real life as Curtis James Jackson III), in a dispute with rapper "Rick Ross" (known in real life as William Leonard Roberts II) over a mixtape Roberts created that borrowed a portion of Jackson's (50 Cent's) hit single, "In Da Club." The problem for Jackson was that he owned no part of the copyrights to the song and the song recording (the copyrights were owned by his record company), so he was forced to challenge Roberts' use of Jackson's voice performing "In Da Club," as well as the use of Jackson's stage name in the track title identifying that song, as a violation of Jackson's right of publicity under Connecticut common law. However, the district court and the Second Circuit concluded that Jackson's claims were preempted under both the doctrine of implied preemption and express preemption of § 301 of the Copyright Act because the pursuit of the claims would impair the ability of a copyright holder or licensee to exploit the rights guaranteed under the Copyright Act.[8] In the case of 50 Cent, the publicity claims were "preemptively" preempted, because the owner of the copyrights associated with the song and recording of Jackson singing "In Da Club" were not seeking to exploit the copyrights and were not even part of the lawsuit, but apparently tolerated Roberts' use of the copyrighted material.

Thus, the copyright preemption doctrine means that if the conflict between the actors', athletes', or celebrities' publicity rights would undermine a copyright owner's rights over the creative expressive work, meaning that the rights asserted under the right of publicity claim (i.e., "You copied my image and likeness, and the appearance of my performance") are the same as claims encompassed by the copyright over the creative expressive work (i.e., "You copied my image and likeness, and the appearance of my performance in a copyrighted work owned by someone else"), then copyright preemption applies.[9] Therefore, when a likeness has been captured in a copyrighted visual work and the work itself is being copied and further distributed, a publicity-right claim interferes with the exclusive rights of the copyright holder, and is preempted by section 301 of the Copyright Act.[10]

But not every attribute of a performer is captured in the recordings of works in which they performed. The

---

[8] *See In re Jackson*, 972 F.3d 25, 34–36 (2d Cir. 2020).

[9] *See* 17 U.S.C. § 301.

[10] *Maloney*, 853 F.3d at 1011; *Dryer*, 814 F.3d at 943; *Jules Jordan Video*, 617 F.3d at 1153–54.

Hoffman case[11] recognized that Dustin Hoffman maintained separate attributes of persona beyond his single appearance as a character in the motion picture, *Tootsie*. Los Angeles Magazine had not obtained from the owners of the rights to the motion picture, *Tootsie*, copyright permission to use a still image of Hoffman's character taken from the copyrighted motion picture, but if they had, it would have brought the case within the copyright preemption sphere.

In the *Midler* and *Waits* cases,[12] Ford Motor Company and Frito-Lay respectively had obtained the copyright license to use the musical compositions (the songs themselves) of Bette Midler and Tom Waits, but did not obtain the separate right of publicity-related right to mimic the sound of their voices singing those same compositions. Nor did Ford or Frito-Law obtain a license to rebroadcast a copyrighted recording that already featured the voices of Midler and Waits, but if they had, it would have precluded publicity claims regarding the use of the recordings under copyright preemption.

In *Facenda v. N.F.L. Films, Inc.*,[13] the National Football League (NFL) owned copyrights to NFL films featuring the distinctive voice-over narration of plaintiff Facenda, but this did not automatically

---

[11] *Hoffman v. Capital Cities/ABC, Inc.*, 255 F.3d 1180 (9th Cir. 2001).

[12] *Midler v. Ford Motor Co.*, 849 F.2d 460 (9th Cir. 1988); *Waits v. Frito-Lay, Inc.*, 978 F.2d 1093 (9th Cir. 1992).

[13] *Facenda v. N.F.L. Films, Inc.*, 542 F.3d 1007, 1028 (3d Cir. 2008).

allow NFL to license the distinctive sound of the announcer's voice that the NFL's licensee attempted to replicate so as to make new voice-over narration for a documentary program on the making of Electronic Arts' Madden NFL Football simulation computer game. In other words, the new work was not merely rebroadcasting preexisting recorded voiceover narration, it was attempting to create new voiceover narration that mimicked the distinctive sound of Facenda's voice, which was directly analogous to *Midler* and *Waits*, where Ford and Frito-Lay attempted to create a new recording of songs using singers who could mimic the sound of Bette Midler's and Tom Waits' singing voices.

LICENSES AND REPUTATION

Copyright licenses can work a similar limitation on publicity claims that draw from the moral rights theory of protection of personality. Under this theory, actions that call into question the dignity and respect of a celebrity or her work might be questioned because they reflect negatively on the celebrity's persona. But not if the action is part of the rights licensed under a copyright agreement.

The disputes of *No Doubt v. Activision,*[14] and *Love v. Activision*[15] both involved rock music simulation

---

[14] *No Doubt v. Activision Publishing, Inc.*, 122 Cal. Rptr. 3d 397, 400 (App. Ct. 2011).

[15] *See* Gus Mastrapa, *Courtney Love Calls Guitar Hero 5's Creepy Cobain 'Vile'*, Wired (Sep. 10, 2009 03:49 PM); Sean Michaels, *Courtney Love to sue over Kurt Cobain Guitar Hero appearance*, The Guardian (Sep. 10, 2009 06.54 PM), https://www.theguardian.com/music/2009/sep/10/courtney-love-kurt-cobain.

video games called *Guitar Hero* and *Band Hero* that were produced by the video game maker, Activision.[16]

In these games, you can cause an avatar of your favorite singers and musicians to rock out to their hits. At advanced levels of the game, after "unlocking" certain avatars, you can cause these same avatars of famous musicians or bands to virtually perform other band's music. For example, you can unlock the Gwen Stefani or Kurt Cobain avatars and have the virtual Stefani or Cobain rock out to *Air Supply* or *The Rolling Stones*' songs. This may sound like a fun evening to a gamer, but it is dreadful sacrilege to some persons near and dear to the original groups, including Courtney Love, the surviving partner and self-proclaimed heir of Kurt Cobain, and the *No Doubt* band members, who have strong objections to even the virtual, simulated use

---

[16] Thumbnail-size excerpt of cover art for Activision's Band Hero Video Game (2015).

of Cobain or members[17] of *No Doubt* playing and singing other bands' songs.[18]

Stefani

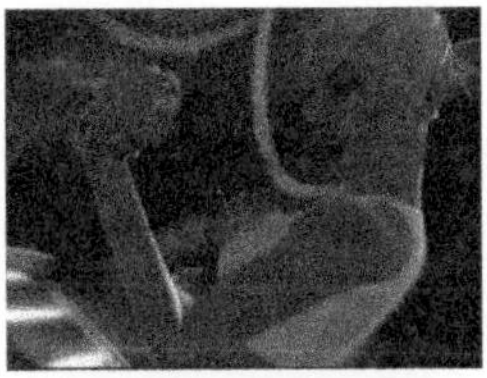

Stefani Avatar

Cobain

Cobain Avatar

The artists' or their heirs' right of publicity claims were undercut by the copyright licenses given to Activision for the use of the musicians' images, likenesses, names, sound of their singing voice, and

[17] Thumbnail-size excerpts Depicting the Parties in Claims against Activision, including Gwen Stefani of No Doubt, and the Avatar of Stefani by Activision, and Kurt Cobain of Nirvana, and the Avatar of Cobain by Activision (2015).

[18] *No Doubt*, 122 Cal. Rptr. 3d at 398–400; Mark Milian, *Courtney Love and Nirvana members unhappy with Kurt Cobain in Guitar Hero*, Pop & Hiss, L.A. Times Music Blog (Sep. 10, 2009, 7:57 pm), https://latimesblogs.latimes.com/music_blog/2009/09/courtney-love-kurt-cobain-guitar-hero-twitter.html.

attributes of their performances. Courtney Love and the *No Doubt* band members had signed off on the contracts that licensed all of these things to Activision. As noted above, the claims raised about the "unlocked" avatars were more akin to "moral rights" claims—that the unlocking and allowing of the avatars to perform other bands' music created a new performance (albeit, usually a very private one, in the video game player's own home) that could be detrimental to the performers' reputations. It was a right to artistic integrity and legacy, threatened by these new performances with completely different music. No Doubt survived a motion to dismiss the suit,[19] and Activision subsequently settled with No Doubt (the terms, as usual, are not disclosed),[20] while Courtney Love never actually sued, and apparently backed down after she reportedly lost control over Kurt Cobain's publicity rights (and other parts of his estate) to Cobain's daughter.[21]

---

[19] *No Doubt*, 122 Cal. Rptr. 3d at 400.

[20] Eriq Gardner, *No Doubt, Activision Settle Lawsuit Over Avatars in 'Band Hero'*, The Hollywood Reporter (Oct. 30, 2012, 3:38 PM), http://www.hollywoodreporter.com/thr-esq/no-doubt-activision-lawsuit-band-hero-376217.

[21] Courtney Garcia, *Courtney Love's interest in Kurt Cobain fades as she reportedly loses control of his image rights*, NBC News, Entertainment (May 3, 2012, 8:11 AM), https://www.nbcnews.com/pop-culture/pop-culture-news/courtney-loves-interest-kurt-cobain-fades-she-reportedly-loses-control-flna1c9386105; Sean Michaels, *Courtney Love loses rights to Kurt Cobain's image*, The Guardian (May 3, 2012, 6.20 PM), https://www.theguardian.com/music/2012/may/03/courtney-love-kurt-cobain.

CHAPTER 8

FALSE ENDORSEMENT AND FALSE DESIGNATION OF ORIGIN

Federal law contains two claims that parallel and sometimes overlap state law right of publicity claims: false endorsement or false designation of origin claims. The source of both of these claims is federal trademark law, section 43(a) of the Lanham Act, codified at 15 U.S.C. § 1125(a). The section provides:

> (a) Civil action
>
> (1) Any person who, on or in connection with any goods or services, or any container for goods, uses in commerce any word, term, name, symbol, or device, or any combination thereof, or any false designation of origin, false or misleading description of fact, or false or misleading representation of fact, which—
>
> (A) is likely to cause confusion, or to cause mistake, or to deceive as to the affiliation, connection, or association of such person with another person, or as to the origin, sponsorship, or approval of his or her goods, services, or commercial activities by another person, . . .[1]

The prohibition about false representation about sponsorship or endorsement includes the implied endorsement of a celebrity for the product or service in connection with which the celebrity's name, image, or likeness is used. This is the part that parallels a

---

[1] 15 U.S.C. § 1125(a).

typical right of publicity claim—use of a name, image, or likeness, without consent or authorization, for some kind of commercial advantage. The federal claim requires that the use be "in commerce," which implies that there are certain uses in the arts, in news media, in education, or other non-commercial activities, that will not fall within the coverage of the federal claim. The federal claim also requires "likelihood of confusion," which asks "whether a reasonably prudent consumer in the marketplace is likely to be confused" with regard to the implied endorsement or sponsorship of the celebrity.

"Likelihood of confusion" considers several factors which vary in number and specific description from circuit to circuit in the federal court system, but the list generally includes factors such as these (from the Ninth Circuit[2]):

1. The level of recognition that the celebrity has among the segment of the society to whom the defendant's product is marketed;

2. The relatedness of the fame or success of the celebrity to the defendant's product;

3. The similarity of the likeness used by the defendant to the actual appearance of the celebrity;

4. Evidence of actual confusion;

---

[2] *Fifty-Six Hope Rd. Music, Ltd. v. A.V.E.L.A., Inc.*, 778 F.3d 1059, 1069 (9th Cir.), *cert. denied*, 577 U.S. 957 (2015); *Downing v. Abercrombie & Fitch*, 265 F.3d 994, 1007–08 (9th Cir. 2001).

5. Marketing channels used;

6. Likely degree of purchaser care;

7. Defendant's intent on selecting the celebrity; and

8. Likelihood of expansion of the product lines.

Examples of (alleged) false endorsement include:

<table>
<tr>
<td>
</td>
<td>Hoffman v. Capital Cities/ABC, Inc., 255 F.3d 1180 (9th Cir. 2001): Dustin Hoffman sued for false endorsement from Los Angeles Magazine's use of his image from his role as the cross-dressing "Tootsie," that was digitally-altered to wear current fashions by Richard Tyler and Ralph Lauren. Hoffman initially prevailed on his Lanham Act, section 43(a) claim at the trial court, but the case was reversed at the Ninth Circuit because the court found that the magazine had included the altered photograph in an article commenting on the upcoming season's fashions, and not in an advertisement (i.e., not commercial speech) for the clothing.</td>
</tr>
</table>

 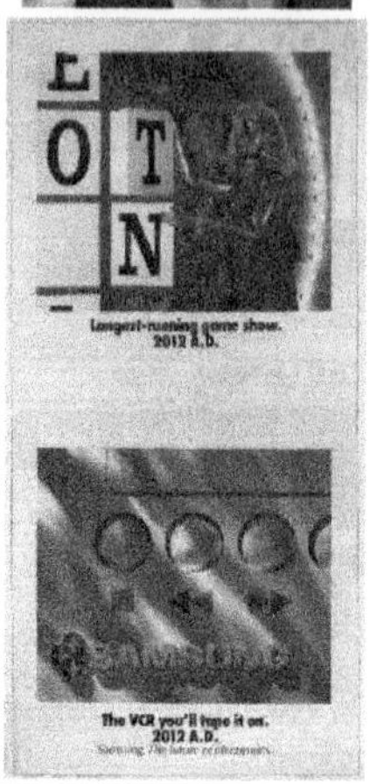	***White v. Samsung Elecs. Am., Inc.***, 971 F.2d 1395, 1400 (9th Cir. 1992), *as amended* (Aug. 19, 1992): *Wheel of Fortune* gameshow television star, Vanna White, sued Samsung for "portraying" White's image and persona as a mechanical robot on a mocked-up *Wheel of Fortune* set in an advertisement for Samsung video cassette recorders. The court accepted the claim under section 43(a) of the Lanham Act because of White's star power and association with television and products, such as Samsung's VCR, that are associated with television.
 	***Waits v. Frito-Lay, Inc.***, 978 F.2d 1093 (9th Cir. 1992): Frito-Lay hired a singer to mimic the raspy dry sound of Waits' singing voice in an ad for Doritos. Waits prevailed on section 43(a) claim of false endorsement.

<table>
<tr><td>

</td><td>Abdul-Jabbar v. General Motors Corp., 85 F.3d 407 (9th Cir. 1996): General Motors used footage of Abdul-Jabbar playing college basketball (under the name Lew Alcindor) in an advertisement for Oldsmobile 88 cars that ran during the March 1993 NCAA tournament. Although he no longer used the name “Lew Alcindor,” the court still upheld Abdul-Jabbar’s Lanham Act, section 43(a) claim for unauthorized use of his name and image in a commercial advertisement.</td></tr>
<tr><td>
</td><td>ETW Corp. v. Jireh Pub., Inc., 332 F.3d 915, 924–25 (6th Cir. 2003): Tiger Woods (ETW) sued Rick Rush (Jireh) in a trademark claim of false endorsement and false designation of origin under section 43(a) of the Lanham Act. The court recognized that Woods could bring the claim as a federal false endorsement claim, but ultimately, the court lumped this claim with the Ohio Right of Publicity statutory claims, and disposed of all</td></tr>
</table>

	publicity-related claims under the theory that the First Amendment permitted Rick Rush to create an artistic expression of the historic significance of Woods' Masters victory (and sell 5000 of these expressions for profit).[3]

Although the "use in commerce" and "likelihood of confusion" elements of the Lanham Act, section 43(a) claim do add steps to the analysis, the outcomes of federal false endorsement claims parallel the outcomes in state law right of publicity claims. A defendant who merely conjures up the persona of a celebrity and creates the possibility of a false express or implied representation that a particular person has authorized or approved use of a product is subject to liability. It is not necessary to use the celebrity's name or actual appearance in the ad.[4]

FALSE DESIGNATION OF ORIGIN

False designation of origin claims under section 43(a) of the Lanham Act seek to prevent false or misleading identifications of the source or origin of

---

[3] Tiger Wood's false designation of origin claim is discussed below in this chapter.

[4] *E.g.*, *Carson v. Here's Johnny Portable Toilets*, 698 F.2d 831 (6th Cir. 1983) (used catch phrase "Here's Johnny," and reference to his role as a "comedian); *White v. Samsung Elecs. Am., Inc.*, 971 F.2d 1395, 1400 (9th Cir. 1992), *as amended* (Aug. 19, 1992) (used robotic facsimile of White's appearance on the gameshow, *Wheel of Fortune*).

goods, and protect the distinguishing value and quality associated with the marks and branding of product producers. As with false endorsement, false designation of origin is a consumer protection-type claim. With celebrities' personality rights, the claim is somewhat complicated to distinguish from the partner claim—also in section 43(a)—of false endorsement, but in false designation of origin, the celebrity should be deeply involved in marketing and selling their own image (their own "brand") in goods, services, and product lines. In that way, a use of the celebrity's name, image, or likeness could be confusing if it suggested that the second user's goods actually came from the product lines and "brands" owned by and associated with the celebrity.

There are three basic kinds of false designation of origin actions:

Passing Off—which refers to a junior user making it appear that his goods are the goods of a more senior producer.[5] Typically, this is done because the senior user's goods are more valuable and desirable, so the junior user reaps a benefit by selling more of his own goods to consumers who are confused into thinking that they actually are buying goods from the senior producer. With a celebrity brand, one might use references or images that could cause consumers to confuse, for example, a junior user's table top grill with a genuine "George Forman" grill, or confuse

---

[5] *See* 15 U.S.C. § 1125(a); *Boston Duck Tours, LP v. Super Duck Tours, LLC*, 531 F.3d 1, 12 (1st Cir. 2008); *Custom Mfg. & Eng'g, Inc. v. Midway Servs., Inc.*, 508 F.3d 641, 647 (11th Cir. 2007).

their own lemonade and ice tea beverage with a licensed "Arnold Palmer" beverage.

Celebrity Branded Products[6]

Reverse Passing Off—refers to a junior user selling the actual goods of a senior user but under the name and mark of the junior user.[7] This may sound incongruous—it will cost the junior user something to be able to obtain the actual goods of a senior user, so why would you sell more expensive goods under your own mark when your own goods cost less? The answer is that this strategy builds up your mark and strengthens the association of your mark with valuable and desirable goods. Eventually, this will raise the perception of quality and value of all goods that are branded with your mark. That works to your advantage, but at the cost of tricking the consumer.

---

[6] Thumbnail-size images of the "George Foreman" Electric Grill, and "Arnold Palmer" Ice Tea and Lemonade Drink.

[7] *See* 15 U.S.C. §§ 1125(a); *Dastar Corp. v. Twentieth Century Fox Film Corp.*, 539 U.S. 23, 27 (2003); *Kehoe Component Sales Inc. v. Best Lighting Products, Inc.*, 796 F.3d 576, 586–87 (6th Cir. 2015), *reh'g denied* (Sept. 14, 2015).

In this case, it is not that the consumers received less than they thought they were bargaining for—the junior user didn't pass off shoddy goods as valuable goods—but the consumer was confused into thinking they were buying one thing but were buying another. The confusion may continue—the next time consumers go shopping they may look for the junior brand thinking that the junior brand stands for something good and desirable, when in fact the junior brand-owner falsely created that impression by the reverse passing off of other's goods as its own.[8]

Misbranding or Mislabeling—the last kind is a more straightforward kind of fraud or misrepresentation: the goods may be fine, but the designation on the label is not.[9] It may not confuse the goods of a senior user with those of a junior user, but somehow the label is misbranded or mislabeled to confuse the origin or contents of the goods, perhaps to confuse or obfuscate their geographic origin, and a consumer will not be getting what they intended to get when they selected the item.[10] Labels like "Organic" or "Green" or "Fat Free" often become so popular as designators that an organization or

---

[8] *See, e.g., Dastar*, 539 U.S. at 27 (Dastar alleged to be improperly reverse passing off film created by Twentieth Century Fox as its own product); *Kehoe Component Sales*, 796 F.3d at 580, 586–87 (appellant manufacturer accused of copying a former collaborator's products and marketing the cloned products as its own).

[9] *See* 15 U.S.C. §§ 1125(a), 1127 (various definitions regarding labeling, tagging of products in commerce); *POM Wonderful LLC v. Coca-Cola Co.*, 573 U.S. 102 (2014); *Lexmark Int'l, Inc. v. Static Control Components, Inc.*, 572 U.S. 118 (2014).

[10] *See* 15 U.S.C. §§ 1125(a), 1127.

regulatory body, such as the United States Food and Drug Administration, must step in to define and regulate what products get to be called "organic" or "fat free" so as to prevent cheaters from adopting a label falsely just to gain the popularity factor. With many goods, geographic indications are a valuable identifier—for example, they separate true Champagne produced in the Champagne region of France from other sparkling wines from other regions across the world. A California Champagne is a misnomer, and a faked geographic indication would certainly cause confusion in the marketplace.[11]

Logos for branded products that are based on a person's name, moniker, or appearance are not uncommon as shown in the following examples

[11] Four thumbnail images of geographic origin designation logos (2015).

featuring Jerry West, Michael Jordan, and Shaquille O'Neal:[12]

A junior user could mislabel their product with an NBA (Jerry West) logo, Michael Jordan logo, or Shaq logo, which would give the confusing impression that the product was an officially endorsed and sponsored product.

In *ETW Inc. v. Jireh Publishing*,[13] in addition to the false endorsement claim discussed in the table above, Tiger Woods also asserted a trademark claim of false designation of origin. The gist of the claim was that the use of an image of Tiger Woods is a use of the Tiger Woods brand. Tiger asserted, in effect, that he is a walking, talking trademark that symbolizes all of the products he is associated with. He himself, and all photographs and images of himself, all are designators of the Tiger Woods brand. And Jireh and Mr. Rush mislabeled their product as being a Tiger

---

[12] Thumbnail-size depictions of trademarked Jerry West Logo for the NBA, Air Jordan "Jumpman" Logo for Nike, Shaquille O'Neal "Shaq Dunkman" Logo for Shaq Brand and for Reebok.

[13] *ETW Corp.*, 332 F.3d at 924–25.

Woods product when they put three images of Tiger on the product.

The false designation of origin claim failed because the court found that Tiger had not used one singular image or any particular image of himself as a designator of goods in commerce. No single image of Tiger had ever been used on goods, on packaging, on the displays and advertising, at the point of purchase for any goods produced by or associated with the Tiger Woods (ETW) Corporation. Thus, a work bearing a portrait of Tiger Woods could not be confused with products from a source or origin that used a particular image of Woods as a mark of the source or original of goods of a certain quality.

The lesson is that celebrities and sports figures cannot claim their persons—and all images of their persons—as a mark. Some persons might be able to use a limited number of images of themselves as marks if they go through all of the requirements of trademark law: adoption of the image (one single image) as a mark, and use of that mark in commerce as an identifier of goods on packaging, on the displays and advertising, at the point of purchase. And then do the same thing for the next individual image, and so on. The incidental verbal references to Tiger Woods by name that appeared in Rick Rush's work and in the packaging of the work were permitted because they were an honest, factual identifier of the subject matter of the prints. Rush was permitted to identify the subject of his painting as a classic, nominal fair use.

What do you do next when your trademark false designation of origin claims fail? You learn from your initial mistakes and try to create and use an actual mark for your goods and services:[14]

Here, Tiger Woods has selected several singular, stylized logos and images and has used them as an identifier of goods or services in commerce. In trademark law terms, these logos and images have been adopted and used a mark. Several of Tiger's new logos involve a stylized T over W design that vaguely

---

[14] Thumbnail-size depictions of "Tiger Woods" and "TW" Trademarked Logos for Tiger Woods Branded goods and services (2017). Disclaimer: No part of this book is endorsed or sponsored by Tiger Woods. These images are merely used to illustrate the celebrity branding of goods or services that could give rise to a false designation of origin claim.

suggests a golf "tee," as well as a sharp tooth, such as the tooth of a tiger.

COPYRIGHT LIMITS ON FALSE DESIGNATION OF ORIGIN CLAIMS

Copyright law imposes limitations on trademark law just as it imposes limits on right of publicity law (*see* Chapter 7, *supra*). The three primary areas of intellectual property rights, copyright, patent, and trademark law, sometimes overlap to protect a project or activity: an invention protected by patent law can have separable decorative elements and written descriptions or depictions protected by copyright and simultaneously lead to an image or logo that is used as a trademark for the goods produced under the patent. However, where one intellectual property has drawn a line precluding protection over a certain endeavor for public policy reasons, another intellectual property will often be precluded from providing an end run around the limitation for the same public policy reasons.

A good example of this effect of copyright law is seen in the United States Supreme Court's opinion in *Dastar v. Twentieth Century Fox.*[15] Dastar took film footage of World War II campaigns that Twentieth Century Fox (TCF) had collected and prepared. Under copyright law, Dastar was well within its rights because TCF's copyright over the footage and the compilation had not been renewed and the footage was now in the public domain, free for all

[15] *Dastar Corp. v. Twentieth Century Fox Film Corp.*, 539 U.S. 23, 28 (2003).

including Dastar to use for any purpose. Dastar's purpose was to edit the footage down to a shorter form and repackage and sell it as a Dastar product: Dastar's "World War II—Campaigns in Europe" sold at or around the fiftieth anniversary of the World War II years.[16]

TCF was not happy. TCF sued Dastar—not for copyright infringement, because the footage had been taken freely from the public domain—but for trademark false designation of origin. The gist of the claim was that Dastar was selling the film footage in commerce under a label that said it was a Dastar product, suggesting that Dastar was the one that took the footage or compiled it. This was alleged to be a false designation of the origin of the product, because TCF was the origin of the product, or at least

[16] Thumbnail excerpt of image of Dastar's "World War II Campaigns in Europe" video collection, the subject of *Dastar Corp. v. Twentieth Century Fox Film Corp.*, 539 U.S. 23, 28 (2003).

the origin of the valuable, expressive contents of the product.

The Supreme Court rejected TCF's false designation of origin claim. The reason was that copyright law had divested TCF of its rights in the works—that is the concept of the public domain; the original creator of the expressive content no longer has rights in the expressive content. TCF's trademark claim for false designation origin was perceived as an attempted "end run" around the limitations imposed by copyright law and its concept of the public domain. This, the Supreme Court would not allow. Trademark is not an alternate route—not an "end run"—around limitations specifically imposed by copyright and patent laws.

Copyrights and patents are true intellectual property rights (also constitution-based rights in U.S. Const. art. I § 8, cl. 8) meant to reward and encourage ingenuity and originality of creativeness. Once the right expires, and Congress has not provided for a revival or extension, the works are meant to go into the public domain where the expressive creations and inventions are free for all.

The Court specifically answered the question, what does "origin" mean in a false designation of origin sense? "Origin" means the source of goods—the actual producer of the goods—not the source of ideas and the expressive, creative content present in the goods. The origin does not mean whose expressions are reflected in the works, even though purchasers may want to know it. *Dastar* concluded that persons cannot wrap new intellectual property protection over public domain works through a Lanham Act § 43(a) claim.[17]

In the celebrity context, this may preclude certain false designation of origin claims regarding works that are copyrighted and contain the names, images, and personas of actors or musicians whose appearances and performances in the film are used in the actual branding and marketing of the works themselves.[18] For example, trailers are created which depict the images and likenesses of the stars acting in the work itself, and are used for purely commercial advertising purposes.

Issues regarding the exploitation of publicity rights certainly can and should be covered by contract as part of the compensation and "residuals" of the actor's contract when the actor agrees to perform in the motion picture. But absent a contract provision

[17] *Dastar Corp.*, 539 U.S. at 28–30.

[18] Thumbnail-size images of Star Wars marketing logos and advertising bearing the images of celebrities starring in the Star Wars motion picture series.

on the topic, a person who seeks a license to create a "Han Solo" or "Luke Skywalker" doll—recurring characters in the Star Wars series—will negotiate with the copyright holders of the Star Wars franchise, presumably Lucasfilm or Disney, and not with the individual stars, Harrison Ford and Mark Hamill, who portrayed those characters in the copyrighted motion pictures. Unless Ford and Hamill bargained for the rights to control their personas in those characters in secondary uses such as toys, they would not have a claim for false designation of origin regarding products based on the characters which were produced under a license from the copyright holders of the Star Wars franchise.

CHAPTER 9

FAIR USE OF CELEBRITY NAMES, IMAGES, AND LIKENESSES

The need to balance free speech rights with publicity rights has led to the creation of a doctrine of fair use in right of publicity law. Celebrities are interesting subjects, and their names, images, personas, and aspects of their lives and performances have symbolic, moral, entertainment, and informational value in expression. All judges, legislators, practitioners, and law professors agree that there are fair uses of celebrities' names, images, and likenesses that do not subject the user to liability for violating a celebrity's right of publicity. There is no question that certain uses fulfill public policy needs and objectives that surpass the need to protect the commercial exploitation value of a celebrity's image or likeness. There even is general agreement on the types of fair uses—news and public affairs reporting, commentary on and criticism of the celebrity, and artistic expression are the main examples. However, the courts in the several states and the different circuits of the federal courts of appeals do not agree on the standards for evaluating what is fair, which leads to uncertainty and unpredictability in evaluating whether a particular use is or will be considered fair.

NEWS AND PUBLIC AFFAIRS, AND ADVERTISING BY NEWS MEDIA

A major limitation on publicity rights comes from the First Amendment's protection of news reporting and dissemination of public affairs information. All sources indicate that news and public affairs reporting is a worthy public interest activity that allows the publication of names, images, and likenesses of celebrities on a regular basis. The activity must actually report current or at least recent or recently acquired information about the celebrity,[1] but beyond that, the category is broad. Just about anything that might be of interest to the public concerning a celebrity counts—and celebrities are classic public figures whose private lives are subject to scrutiny and exposure by media, which significantly limits the protection of publicity and privacy claims.

In general, news and public interest media outlets will have broad discretion in how they communicate the name, image, or likeness of a "celebrity" in a news story or other form of public interest communication, even when the information is delivered in an "infotainment" format such as a "docudrama." In the

---

1 *Compare Toffoloni v. LFP Publ'g Grp., LLC*, 572 F.3d 1201, 1213 (11th Cir. 2009) (publication of twenty-year-old images of murdered wrestler were not protected by newsworthiness defense), *with Brown v. Showtime Networks, Inc.*, 394 F. Supp. 3d 418, 437–38 (S.D.N.Y. 2019) (right of publicity claim failed because images of pop icon Whitney Houston's daughter were held to be newsworthy and a matter of "public interest" regarding the depiction of Houston's familial relationships in her life story).

recent case of *Porco v. Lifetime Entertainment*,[2] convicted murderer Chris Porco, named "The Romeo Killer" by the media, challenged the "ripped from the headlines" biopic of his life and crime created and aired by Lifetime Entertainment on the grounds that the biopic was "substantially fictionalized," and thus forfeited the newsworthiness defense. The trial court agreed, but on appeal, the New York Appellate Division court reversed. The appellate court accepted that Lifetime could tell the facts of the story but still use standard devices that fictionalize parts of the facts to make it a better, more coherent story. It is common for unauthorized biographies, biopics, and historical fiction to combine events, invent scenes, and create "composite characters" to smooth over gaps in the record. The court allowed that Lifetime could use flashbacks, staged interviews, and imagined dialogue so long as the underlying event was newsworthy (as it was in the *Romeo Killer* docudrama) and the work provided a "broadly accurate description" of those events (which the *Romeo Killer* docudrama did).

The news and public affairs power carries over to commercial speech when media outlets wish to advertise their publications. A successful occupation of publishing genuine news and juicy scandal about celebrities can be advertised, and the advertisements for the news and public affairs publication can feature some of the images and likenesses of celebrities that have been "covered" in the past. This

---

[2] *Porco v. Lifetime Ent. Servs.*, LLC, 150 N.Y.S.3d 380 (App. Div. 3d Dep't), *appeal dismissed*, 177 N.E.3d 589 (N.Y. 2021).

point should be noted: even though uses of celebrity images in commercial advertising is the paradigmatic right of publicity claim that celebrities *win*, the tables are turned when the advertising is of a previous protected use, such as a use in a bona fide news or public interest reporting context.

In *Booth v. Curtis Publishing Company*,[3] Shirley Booth,[4] a well-known actress (at the time), brought an action against the defendant publisher for the unauthorized use of her image in a magazine and subsequent use in another medium as an advertisement for the first publication. The pictures were taken by a photographer of a travel magazine while the actress was on vacation in Jamaica. The photos were later published in the travel magazine and then used as a part of an advertisement for the magazine. The New York court held that the use of the actress's image in this instance was protected by

---

[3] *Booth v. Curtis Pub. Co.*, 223 N.Y.S.2d 737 (App. Div.), *aff'd*, 182 N.E.2d 812 (N.Y. 1962).

[4] Thumbnail-size excerpt of image depicting Shirley Booth, the subject of the case, *Booth v. Curtis Pub. Co.*, 223 N.Y.S.2d 737 (App. Div.), *aff'd*, 182 N.E.2d 812 (N.Y. 1962).

the First Amendment of the U.S. Constitution. Addressing the original photograph, published by a travel magazine, the court held that the reproduction was for news purposes; therefore, it was not a violation of New York's privacy and publicity law, N.Y. Civil Rights Law §§ 50, 51. Furthermore, the court held that the republication of the photograph as an advertisement of the magazine also was permissible. The court held that the reproduction of the photos was allowable as long as it was incidental advertising of the news medium. The court explained that a publication can best prove its worth through an extraction from past editions.[5]

In *Namath v. Sports Illustrated*,[6] Sports Illustrated used a picture of Joe Namath, with his consent, in an

---

[5] *Booth,* 223 N.Y.S.2d at 744–45.

[6] *Namath v. Sports Illustrated,* 371 N.Y.S.2d 10 (App. Div. 1975), *aff'd*, 352 N.E.2d 584 (N.Y. 1976).

issue of the magazine.[7] Namath sued when, later, Sports Illustrated republished the picture as an advertisement of the magazine. The court held, where the use of a professional athlete's photograph was merely incidental to advertising of a publisher's magazine in which the athlete had earlier been properly and fairly depicted, and the language of the advertisement did not indicate the athlete's endorsement of the magazine, there was no invasion of the athlete's right to privacy or publicity in violation of N.Y. Civil Rights Law.[8]

The Ninth Circuit Court of Appeals followed similar reasoning in *Cher v. Forum International, Ltd.*[9] In

[7] Thumbnail-size excerpt of Sports Illustrated Cover depicting Joe Namath, the subject of the case, *Namath v. Sports Illustrated*, 371 N.Y.S.2d 10 (App. Div. 1975), *aff'd*, 352 N.E.2d 584 (N.Y. 1976).

[8] *Namath,* 371 N.Y.S.2d at 11.

[9] *Cher v. Forum Int'l, Ltd.*, 692 F.2d 634 (9th Cir. 1982). Thumbnail-size excerpt of *Forum* Magazine cover depicting Cher,

this case, Cher, a well-known actress and singer, sued a free-lance writer who conducted an interview with her for *Us* magazine. Later, Cher and *Us* agreed that the article would not run in *Us* magazine. The free-lance writer then sold the article or portions of the article to *Star* magazine and *Forum*. Cher sued for exploitation of her celebrity value to sell magazines without her consent by implied endorsement. The court stated that constitutional protection extends to the truthful use of a public figure's name and likeness in advertising which is merely an adjunct of the protected publication and promotes only the protected publication. Furthermore, the court emphasized that advertising to promote a news medium is not actionable under an appropriation of publicity theory so long as the advertising does not falsely claim that the public figure endorses the news medium. However, as to the two defendants who boasted that Cher had told them things that she would "never tell to *People* or to *Us*," the court sustained Cher's action because these defendants had lied.[10]

---

the subject of the case, *Cher v. Forum Int'l, Ltd.*, 692 F.2d 634 (9th Cir. 1982).

[10] *Cher*, 692 F.2d at 638–40.

The newspaper defendant in *Montana v. San Jose Mercury News, Inc.*,[11] reported the San Francisco 49er's Super Bowl victories in 1989 and 1990 with cover photos of the star quarterback, Joe Montana.[12] The newspaper further commemorated the victories with a bonus, "Souvenir Section," with large blow-ups of the celebratory Montana. Then the newspaper created posters of several of the images from the

[11] *Montana v. San Jose Mercury News, Inc.*, 40 Cal. Rptr. 2d 639 (Ct. App. 1995), *as modified* (May 30, 1995).

[12] Thumbnail-size excerpt of cover page photo depicting Joe Montana, the subject of the case, *Montana v. San Jose Mercury News, Inc.*, 40 Cal. Rptr. 2d 639 (Ct. App. 1995), *as modified* (May 30, 1995).

souvenir section, some of which were sold for $5, but the rest were given away. Montana sued, believing no doubt that the newspaper had strayed from its protected status as an outlet of news. The Court stood by the newspaper, stating that the "First Amendment protects [defendant's 49er Super Bowl victory] posters . . . because the posters themselves report newsworthy items of public interest."[13] The newspaper had previously printed a front page story on the San Francisco 49er's multiple Super Bowl victories and in conjunction with that news story, printed a picture featuring the 49er's quarterback Joe Montana. Both the news story itself and Mr. Montana's involvement in it were considered to be newsworthy. The posters merely reprinted the front page of the newspaper's reporting of this newsworthy story. The newspaper did not simply create a poster solely to exploit the image of Joe Montana.[14]

However, even news reporting has its limits. The *Montana* case may be contrasted with *Jordan v. Jewel Food Stores*,[15] which held that a full page work congratulating Michael Jordan on his election to the Basketball Hall of Fame that was created by the owner of Jewel-Osco stores in Chicago and that ran in a commemorative edition of Sports Illustrated devoted to the career of Michael Jordan, was in a fact a commercial advertisement for Jewel-Osco stores

---

[13] *Montana*, 40 Cal. Rptr. 2d at 640–41.

[14] *Id.* at 640–42.

[15] *Jordan v. Jewel Food Stores, Inc.*, 743 F.3d 509, 513–22 (7th Cir. 2014).

because the work prominently featured the stores' name and slogan.[16]

The press has a privilege to report matters of legitimate public interest even though such reports might intrude on matters otherwise private.[17] Images of private citizens who are involved in news stories must be used in a manner directly related to the reporting of the newsworthy event, and not exploited for commercial speech. In *Shulman v. Group W Prods., Inc.*,[18] a car accident victim was

---

[16] Thumbnail-size excerpt of Jewel-Osco ad commemorating Michael Jordan, the subject of the case, *Jordan v. Jewel Food Stores, Inc.*, 743 F.3d 509 (7th Cir. 2014).

[17] *New York Times Co. v. Sullivan*, 376 U.S. 254, 283–84 (1964) (inaccurate but unintentional mistakes in reporting in paid editorial in newspaper was protected from state law defamation suit).

[18] *Shulman v. Grp. W Prods., Inc.*, 955 P.2d 469, 478–79 (Cal. 1998), *as modified on denial of reh'g* (July 29, 1998).

filmed in the hands of an EMT crew. The court held, "The contents of the publication or broadcast are protected only if they have 'some substantial relevance to a matter of legitimate public interest.' "[19] Thus, recent decisions have generally tested newsworthiness with regard to such individuals by assessing the logical relationship or nexus, or the lack thereof, between the events or activities that brought the person into the public eye and the particular facts disclosed.[20]

An approval to use an image for one purpose does not automatically imply that the image can later be used for unrelated purposes, such as commercial speech.[21] In *Robinson v. Snapple Bev. Corp.*,[22] the *Sugar Hill Gang* agreed to appear to promote a charity benefit sponsored by defendant Snapple and the recording artists were filmed at the event. Snapple later used the footage for a commercial advertisement for its soft drink products. The second use was not protected by the first use as the second use was a bare advertisement for commercial merchandise that did

---

[19] *Id.* at 478–79.

[20] *Id. See also D'Andrea v. Rafla-Demetrious*, 972 F. Supp. 154, 156–57 (E.D.N.Y. 1997), *aff'd*, 146 F.3d 63 (2d Cir. 1998) (resident at hospital photographed for promotional brochure; use of image held incidental to purpose of brochure, and thus non-actionable).

[21] *Toney v. L'Oreal USA*, 406 F.3d 905, 908 (7th Cir. 2005) (authorized use of image and likeness for a limited-time ad campaign did not imply continued right to use image and likeness in other campaigns); *Christoff v. Nestle USA*, 213 P.3d 132, 136 (Cal. 2009) (same).

[22] *Robinson v. Snapple Beverage Corp.*, No. 99 CIV. 344 (LMM), 2000 WL 781079 (S.D.N.Y. June 19, 2000).

not relate back to the reporting of any newsworthy event.[23]

MULTIPLE, COMPETING FAIR USE TESTS

Outside the news and public affairs reporting context, there are no less than *five* separate and distinct fair use tests that have been applied by courts in right of publicity cases. All of them speak to the same issue: the proper balance of First Amendment expression and other public policy benefits weighed against the protection of publicity rights.

Cardtoons— Balancing test	10th Cir.	Court is to balance the value of the expression under 1st Amendment against the value of protecting the celebrity name-image-likeness used. *Cardtoons, L.C. v. Major League Baseball Players Ass'n*, 95 F.3d 959, 968–76 (10th Cir. 1996)
Rogers— Relatedness test	2d Cir.	Court is to determine if the use of the celebrity name-image-likeness is directly related to the content of the expression or if instead it is a disguised

23 *Id.* at *4–5.

		advertisement and exploitation. *Rogers v. Grimaldi*, 875 F.2d 994, 999–1005 (2d Cir. 1989)
Comedy III—Transformative test	Cal. Supreme Ct.	Court is to determine if the artist adds value to the depiction beyond the value of the celebrity image either through artistic additions or because of the status of the artist (e.g., Warhol). Asks if people would buy the work for the art/artist or for the celebrity image. *Comedy III Prods., Inc. v. Gary Saderup, Inc.*, 21 P.3d 797, 804–08 (Cal. 2001)
Simeonov—NY Artistic Expression test	N.Y. Civil Ct.	Court ruled that any artist can make and sell a representation of a celebrity if done in "limited numbers." *Simeonov v. Tiegs*, 602 N.Y.S.2d 1014, 1018 (Civ. Ct. N.Y. Cty. 1993)

CBC, Doe— Predominant Purpose test	8th Cir., Mo. Supreme Ct.	Court is to determine if the predominant purpose of the activity is for expressive, artistic, news purposes, or is it predominantly to unfairly exploit the celebrity name-image-likeness. *C.B.C. Distribution & Mktg., Inc. v. Major League Baseball Advanced Media, L.P.*, 505 F.3d 818, 820 (8th Cir. 2007); *Doe v. TCI Cablevision*, 110 S.W.3d 363 (Mo. 2003)

BALANCING TEST

Balancing tests are popular in the law. They are easy to define, and easy to understand. You can identify the factors that are to be balanced, adding or modifying factors as the cases roll along and needs arise to tweak the test. The problem is that balancing tests are terrible tests with which to make predictions about outcomes. The criteria to be balanced, no matter how carefully defined, always lead to a case-by-case determination. If a judge feels that a certain outcome is the best, the judge almost always can make the balancing come out in favor of that outcome. Therefore, lawyers and law professors have to carefully compile the record of cases applying the test to see patterns in successful narratives as well as patterns of unsuccessful narratives.

Cardtoons LC v. Major League Baseball Players Assoc.[24] is a major, early case that adopted and applied a balancing test. *Cardtoons* involved a manufacturer of comic baseball cards that emphasized the more outrageous egos and behaviors of the game's biggest stars.[25] Instead of statistics of batting average, slugging percentage, earned run average, and walks plus hits per inning pitched, the cards talked about lifestyle, personality, and the general inflated arrogance and inflated salaries of many stars. For example, Barry Bonds was identified as "Treasury Bonds" and the Cardtoons card made ironic statements about his salary and his worth through several banking and monetary system puns. The team names and logos were altered, too, to try to match the commentary; e.g., the San Francisco Giants appear as the "Gents" with a fancy top hat as their new logo, although the Giants' orange and black color scheme was maintained in the player picture:

[24] *Cardtoons, L.C. v. Major League Baseball Players Ass'n*, 95 F.3d 959 (10th Cir. 1996).

[25] *Id.* at 963–65.

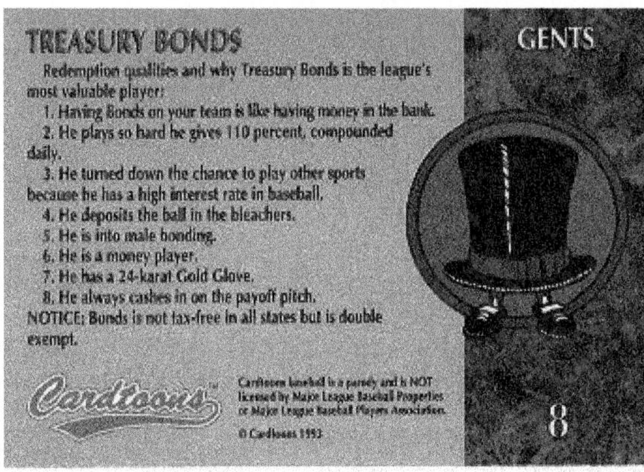

The cards presented a form of humorous commentary on the players.[26] The Cardtoons people printed a

[26] Thumbnail-size excerpt of the front and back of Cardtoon's card depicting a caricature of Barry Bonds, at issue in the case, *Cardtoons, L.C. v. Major League Baseball Players Ass'n*, 95 F.3d 959 (10th Cir. 1996).

disclaimer on the back of the cards: "Cardtoons baseball is a parody and is NOT licensed by Major League Baseball Properties or Major League Baseball Players Association." A disclaimer in the law is not a guaranty that people will leave you alone, or that no one will confuse your work with genuine authorized works of the people whose endorsement you are disclaiming. But in this case, the disclaimer helped the courts to determine that this was a parody, and that it was a bona fide comment on and criticism of the players.

So begins the balancing. In one side of the scale, we place the value of protecting the publicity rights in the context of how they were used or displayed by the defendant. In this case, the publicity rights involved were highly valuable and expensive. Cardtoons had chosen a high value target—professional baseball players—whose publicity values are very high on the food chain for celebrities in general, and for marketing and promotion in particular. And Cardtoons took the best, most famous of the players for their cards. The use was commercial—the cards were being sold—but the use of the images wasn't blatantly commercial in the sense of commercial advertising. The only thing being promoted was the cards themselves. In the other side of the scale, we place the value of the public policies being served by the use. Here, we have two very important, high value public policies: freedom of speech, and the right to criticize public figures. This was tempered by a very practical consideration—that celebrities will never authorize the use of their names, images, or likenesses in a use that criticizes them. It is both contrary to human nature and against the celebrity's business interests to give the green light to someone who wants to take you down a peg. And if the outcome of the case was that a parody spoof of baseball players was not fair, and was a violation of the baseball players' rights of publicity, then this would shut down almost all critical commentary on athletes in particular, and entertainment public figures in general. The loss of criticism of public figures would be viewed as a tremendous loss in our First Amendment jurisprudence, so the scales were tipped in favor of allowing the parody as a fair use. And that is how the case came out.

Cardtoons provides a narrative of success as to how the balancing should work out in situations such as *Cardtoons'* where there is strong First Amendment critical speech involving celebrities and moderate commercial exploitation of the celebrities' persona.

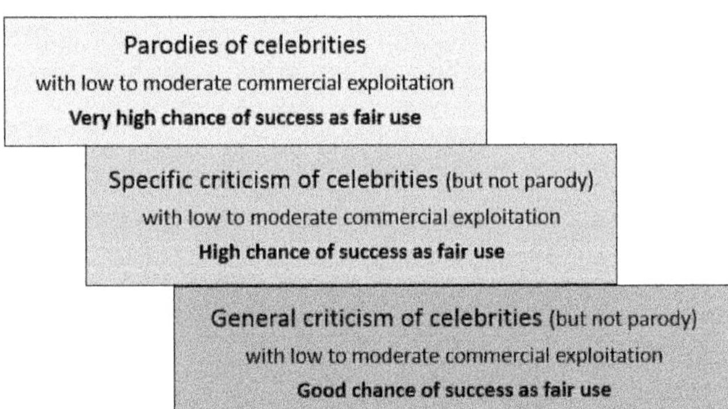

As the situation moves away from classic commentary, and toward more general levels of criticism, the odds of proving a fair use go down. The factors are in play, meaning that if the commercial exploitation appears to be great, as in the case of a product or publication that prominently uses a celebrity name or likeness on its face with little substantive critical commentary, then the balance would tip away from fair use.

Cardtoons is one case; predictions are improved if we have multiple cases to work with. Fortunately, many of the other cases used *Cardtoons*' balancing test as one of their tests of fair use, so we have several other examples of success or failure narratives to look at.

RELATEDNESS TEST

In *Rogers v. Grimaldi*,[27] Federico Fellini, the famous Italian film director, and Alberto Grimaldi, a film producer, made a movie, *Ginger & Fred* (*Ginger e Fred* in Italian), about Argentinian ballroom dancers known in the movie as the "Fred and Ginger of Argentina." Other than the occupation of the aging ballroom dancers, the movie has nothing else in common with the careers of the real "Ginger"—Ginger Rogers, and the real "Fred"—Fred Astaire, the dancing duo of many American 1930s and 40s movie offerings. In Fellini's film, there is no other image or dialogue included about Ginger Rogers, and her picture or likeness was not used in any promotional material for the film. Nevertheless,

---

[27] *Rogers v. Grimaldi*, 875 F.2d 994 (2d Cir. 1989).

Ginger Rogers wanted to protect her persona from exploitation, and believed that her first name in the title of any movie involving ballroom dancing was exploitation enough. She sued Fellini, the director, and Grimaldi, the producer of the film.[28]

The court ruled for Grimaldi and Fellini on the basis of fair use. The court applied a new test (new to the context of right of publicity claims that overlap with the concept of false endorsement trademark claims, at least) referred to as the "relatedness" test:

- In cases involving speech or artistic expression,

---

[28] Thumbnail-size excerpts of photograph depicting Ginger Rogers and Fred Astaire dancing, and an image of Fellini's *Ginger e Fred* motion picture promotion, at issue in *Rogers v. Grimaldi*, 875 F.2d 994 (2d Cir. 1989).

- If the use of a celebrity name or image is directly related to the underlying content and meaning of the expression, the use is fair,
- But if the use is not related to the content of the speech, and it appears that the use might be a disguised advertisement and thus, exploitation, then the use is not fair.[29]

Rogers' relatedness test evaluates the "artistic relevance of the image or name used to the work" and polices whether the use, if not directly related, is therefore "explicitly misleading" as to the source or the content of the work and suggests sponsorship or endorsement of the work by the celebrity.[30] Although, not phrased in exactly this manner, the court is looking for outward exploitation of the image, especially in a manner that looks like commercial advertising or trade dress (trade dress being the packaging or display of products at the point of sale), as opposed to speech or artistic expression that logically discusses or features the celebrity name or image.

In *Rogers*, the court found that Grimaldi and Fellini had a bona fide reason for including the name "Ginger" in the content of the work and in the title of the work—their narrative was about aging ballroom dancers, and it was logical for the fictional pair to have been given a nickname such as Ginger and Fred. Also, the adoption of the nickname alone for the title appeared to be related to the expression, and not

---

[29] *Rogers*, 875 F.2d at 999–1005.

[30] *Id.*

simply used as a marketing ploy to exploit the good name and reputation of Ginger Rogers.[31]

Rogers and *Cardtoons* have been used many times since in right of publicity cases, and often they are used in the same case. The same goes for the next two tests, the "transformative" test and the "artistic expression" test.[32]

TRANSFORMATIVE TEST

From time to time, courts struggling with the concept of fair use in right of publicity law have looked for guidance in other areas of the law that have analogous subject matter and public policy underpinnings as publicity law. Copyright law was an obvious place to look: both publicity law and copyright law are property-law based actions. They have, at least in part, the same public policy of encouraging the development of talent and expertise for the betterment and enrichment of the public at large, and indirectly, for the support of artists and entertainers. Both deal with First Amendment expressive fair uses. So, when the California Supreme Court in *Comedy III Productions v. Gary*

---

[31] *Id.* at 1004–05.

[32] *E.g.*, *In re NCAA Student-Athlete Name & Likeness Licensing Litig.*, 724 F.3d at 1268, and *Hart*, 717 F.3d at 165–70 (discussed *infra* Chapter 10), both considered and rejected several tests—*Rogers*' Relatedness test, *Doe* and *C.B.C. Distribution*'s Predominant Purpose test, and *Cardtoons*' Balancing test—before settling on *Comedy III*'s Transformative test.

Saderup, Inc.,[33] borrowed the transformative test from copyright fair use law, it created an interesting and potentially useful fair use test, but the court applied it in a manner that may set back artists for years in California and other jurisdictions that follow the California Supreme Court's logic in interpreting and applying the test.

The "transformative test" is not as simple and straightforward as the balancing test and the relatedness test. It requires an examination of the use of the name and image of the celebrity, and whether the new work transforms the content and appearance of the celebrity or her persona or aspects of her performance in such a way that the use no longer looks like exploitation, and appears to be more like new expression.

In copyright law, the transformative test works this way:

> [T]he transformative test is used for the evaluation of copyright fair uses, and the test works out to mean that if a person copies a portion or the whole of another artist's or author's creation, then the second user must transform the original work in one of several ways: (a) add new content to the old expression, so that it has new meaning; (b) put the old work into a new context—this is known as "recontextualization," and the new context should be one that changes the overall function,

[33] *Comedy III Prods., Inc. v. Gary Saderup, Inc.*, 21 P.3d 797, 804–08 (Cal. 2001).

> purpose, and meaning of the old work; (c) put the old expression to work for an entirely new function and purpose; or (d) best of all, do two or three of (a), (b), (c) together, to really upend the original work's content, meaning, function, *and* purpose. The idea is not to replicate the original work and show it again for its original expressive purpose and value. If the original shines through in the second work, then the transformation is incomplete and the fair use fails.[34]

There is a basic problem with importing the transformative test from copyright law into right of publicity law: copyright deals with works—paintings, books, films, and other expressive works. Publicity law deals with people. There is not a ready metaphor for *transforming* people and their persona the way that there is for physical, expressive works. We all know of paintings, songs, films, and books that have been altered or adapted. We have less to go on with transformations of celebrity names, images, and likenesses. (I assume the law does not require the kind of transformations that some celebrities engage in, such as with Lady Gaga, Madonna, or David Bowie, who went through many phases in their public personae).

As a replacement for the concept of adaptation, alteration, or recontextualization, *Comedy III* offered

---

[34] *See* Michael D. Murray, *What Is Transformative? An Explanatory Synthesis of the Convergence of Transformation and Predominant Purpose in Copyright Fair Use Law*, 11 CHI.-KENT J. INTELL. PROP. 260, 264 (2012).

the following criteria for what is transformative of a celebrity persona when it appears in another expressive work:

> Primary inquiry: Is the work merely a depiction of the celebrity, no matter how skillfully executed, or did the artist add new creative expression that has value beyond that of the star's image?
>
> Subsidiary inquiry: Would an average member of the public buy the work for the art or the artist, or for the celebrity's image?[35]

Comedy III made "supplementation" and "augmentation" actions of transformation when it comes to depictions involving a celebrity image. The artist must add new creative expression beyond simply applying artistic techniques to render a depiction of the celebrity.[36]

The subsidiary inquiry stated above sets up a potentially difficult standard for new and up-and-coming artists to meet: if a buyer is more like to pick their work because it depicts a certain celebrity than because it is by a particular artist or because of its artistic techniques, then the work fails the transformative test and is not a fair use of the celebrity image.

---

[35] *Comedy III*, 21 P.3d at 809, 810.

[36] *Id.* at 809–11 (finding that the skillful artistic rendering of Saderup's depiction of the Three Stooges in fact does not meet the court's standards of transformation of the appearance of the celebrities).

The test might still sound very workable, especially for well-known artists, but the sour note in the story here is that the California Supreme Court declared that the defendant, an artist by the name of Gary Saderup, had done a skillful, artistic rendering in charcoal of images of the Three Stooges comedy team, and that there was no denying that the work reflected superior artistic skill and technique:[37]

The Three Stooges in *You Natzy Spy*

Saderup's rendering of the Three Stooges

---

[37] Thumbnail-size excerpts of the source material depiction of the Three Stooges in a motion picture promotional image for *You Nazty Spy*, compared to Gary Saderup's depiction of the Three Stooges in the work at issue in *Comedy III Prods., Inc. v. Gary Saderup, Inc.*, 21 P.3d 797 (Cal. 2001).

The court then proceeded to declare that the work was not transformative, and therefore not a fair use.[38] On the subsidiary inquiry, the court found that the work would obviously be purchased by Three Stooges enthusiasts because it depicted the celebrities' images and not by any association of the work with Saderup.[39]

The *Comedy III* court held out Andy Warhol as a prime example of an artist whose uses of famous celebrity images were transformative:[40]

Warhol Celebrity Portraits

---

[38] *Comedy III*, 21 P.3d at 810–11.

[39] *Id.* at 811. Note that Saderup had a small-scale business tied up in charcoal, black-and-white renditions of celebrities. His output included original works and art prints. He was not a purveyor of memorabilia or kitsch merchandise of the t-shirts, towels, aprons, and coffee mug varieties. Yet, his skillfully rendered art or burgeoning reputation were not enough to get him over the transformative test, as interpreted by the California Supreme Court.

[40] Thumbnail-size excerpts of Andy Warhol's portraits of Jackie O, Marilyn Monroe, and Ingrid Bergman, as discussed in the case, *Comedy III Prods., Inc. v. Gary Saderup, Inc.*, 21 P.3d 797, 811 (Cal. 2001).

The example of Warhol suggests that there is a "genius standard" at work in this test—that artists gain the protection of a fair use if the artists' personal fame allows them to sell works for their own artistic value even though they borrow other celebrities' images, but lesser known artists, such as Gary Saderup, must produce something truly unique and creative in order to escape a right of publicity claim.[41]

TRANSFORMATIVE SUCCESSES

Just when you might give up on the transformative test as being hopelessly limited by a genius and superstar standard in California, the California Supreme Court took another case with artistic expression and the claims of celebrities for violation of the right of publicity. In *Winter v. D.C. Comics*,[42] a claim was brought by Johnny and Edgar Winter who

---

[41] It is perhaps noteworthy that two decades after the *Comedy III* opinion of the California Supreme Court, the United States Court of Appeals for the Second Circuit found that Andy Warhol's characteristic depictions of celebrities are *not* transformative, at least in the copyright law incarnation of that fair use test. *Andy Warhol Found. for Visual Arts, Inc. v. Goldsmith*, 11 F.4th 26, 37–44 (2d Cir. 2021). The case involved a series of Warhol's depictions of the rock icon, Prince, that were based on a photograph of Prince taken by Lynn Goldsmith. The claims did not involve right of publicity law and instead arose from Goldsmith's copyright claims against Warhol's foundation. The opinion interpreted and applied the copyright transformative fair use test, but the opinion still undercuts some of the logic of the California Supreme Court's interpretation and application of the right of publicity transformative fair use test in which the California court held that Warhol is a perfect example of an artist whose depictions of celebrities are most definitely transformative in all the right "fair use" senses of the term.

[42] *Winter v. DC Comics*, 69 P.3d 473 (Cal. 2003).

were country singers and brothers known for their very white blonde hair acquired as a result of being albinos.

The D.C. Comic, Jonah Hex, spoofed the two singers by having them appear in the comic as large albino worms with the characteristically white hair, that were named "the Autumn brothers" in the comic. They were featured on at least one cover of the comic (seen below).

Autumn Brothers on the cover of *Jonah Hex* comic

Johnny and Edgar, the Winter Brothers[43]

The Winter brothers sued, but they did not prevail. The California Supreme Court recognized that the

[43] Thumbnail-size excerpts of Jonah Hex comic book cover depicting Autumn Brothers, and a photograph depicting the two Winter Brothers, the subjects of the case, *Winter v. DC Comics*, 69 P.3d 473 (Cal. 2003).

purpose of the work was a parody, and in the course of spoofing the singing duo, the artists and author of the comics engaged in a significant alteration of their appearance.[44] There was a significant amount of recontextualization, too, with the change from twentieth century country performers to supernatural, gun-slinging, "Wild West" era worms. The parody purpose and altered appearance and context were enough to find that the work was transformative and a fair use.

Transformation does not need to involve or accompany parody or mockery to be successful. The Third Circuit case of *Hamilton v. Speight*[45] is the counterpoint to the *Doe v. TCI Cablevision*[46] (use of professional hockey player's name and reputation) and *Hart v. Electronic Arts, Inc.*[47] (use of college football player's persona) cases. In *Hamilton*, Lenwood Hamilton, a former professional football player and wrestler who performed as "Hard Rock Hamilton," sued Epic Games and Microsoft, the creators and owners of the popular video game *Gears of War*. Hamilton's likeness and persona were allegedly used to create a character in *Gears of War* called Augustus "Cole Train" Cole. Contrary to the holdings in *Doe* and *Hart*, court held that the likeness and persona of Lenwood/Hard Rock Hamilton was at best one of the "raw materials" used to create the sum

---

[44] *Winter*, 69 P.3d at 480.

[45] *Hamilton v. Speight*, 413 F. Supp. 3d 423, 428–34 (E.D. Pa. 2019), *aff'd*, 827 F. App'x 238, 239–40 (3d Cir. 2020), *cert. denied*, 141 S. Ct. 2796 (2021).

[46] *Doe v. TCI Cablevision*, 110 S.W.3d 363, 372–73 (Mo. 2003).

[47] *Hart v. Elec. Arts, Inc.*, 717 F.3d 141, 152–55 (3d Cir. 2013).

and substance of the video game character. The court held that the use was transformative and therefore protected under the First Amendment.[48]

ARTISTIC EXPRESSION ALONE

Simeonov v. Tiegs[49] is a peculiar case that happens to have given us one of the most artist-friendly tests for fair use in a right of publicity context: the "artistic expression test." The case takes us back to New York, and its N.Y. Civil Rights Law §§ 50 and 51. But it is a long strange trip to the fair use issue. The case started when Cheryl Tiegs, a former supermodel and cover girl, wanted to help raise money for the preservation of African elephants. A plan was devised to cast an elephant in alginate, a sculpting media used for, among other things, art castings and dental castings. Some persons thought the casting would hurt the elephant. Tiegs thought better, and to prove her point, she arranged for the sculptor on the project, Mihail Simeonov, to make a casting of her own cover model-worthy face. He did so, and no harm came to Tiegs. Point made. The elephant was cast. Simeonov used the casting of Tieg's face to make several bronze sculptures of Tieg's head and shoulders. He lent one to Tiegs to show in her apartment.

---

[48] *Hamilton*, 827 F. App'x at 239–40 (the Third Circuit's opinion that affirmed the District Court's opinion is denoted as "not precedential" according to the court's internal operating procedures).

[49] *Simeonov v. Tiegs*, 602 N.Y.S.2d 1014 (Civ. Ct. N.Y. Cty. 1993).

Cheryl Tiegs

Simeonov bust[50]

Later, when workers were remodeling the apartment, the Simeonov sculpture was damaged. Simeonov sued for damages. Tiegs did not want to pay and asserted a right of publicity defense to the action—arguing that Simeonov did not have permission to create a likeness of Tiegs, and thus could not be compensated for the destruction of an unauthorized infringement. Simeonov thought better, and he claimed a right to create a work of art depicting a celebrity.

For no particular reason other than the First Amendment and the right of free expression, including artistic expression, the court agreed with Simeonov. Far be it from declaring a genius standard, the New York Civil Court (a trial court with limited jurisdiction in New York County) declared that: "any artist can make a recognizable

[50] Thumbnail-size excerpts of portrait of Cheryl Tiegs and a Simeonov bust, the subjects of the case, *Simeonov v. Tiegs*, 602 N.Y.S.2d 1014 (Civ. Ct. N.Y. Cty. 1993).

likeness of a celebrity and make a limited number of copies without violating New York's right of publicity statute."[51] Simeonov had made twenty copies of the sculpture, so presumably twenty is an appropriately limited number.

The *Simeonov* case was issued by the Civil Court of New York City, a limited jurisdiction trial level court in New York, thus it is not precedential (*i.e.*, not controlling authority for other courts in New York), and it is of somewhat limited persuasive power for other jurisdictions to follow. But the case has been followed by several New York courts, including federal courts in New York applying New York law,[52] and thus may be interpreted as accurately stating the law in New York regarding the artistic expression defense to N.Y. Civil Rights Law § 51 right of privacy and publicity claims. Nevertheless, the simplicity of the test has not sold it to other states. It remains on the books and is available to use to make one more argument if you are arguing for an artistic fair use.

PREDOMINANT PURPOSE TEST

Missouri is responsible for making law on the question of the right of publicity fair use analysis:

---

[51] *Simeonov*, 602 N.Y.S.2d at 1018.

[52] The following cases all follow *Simeonov*: *Foster v. Svenson*, 7 N.Y.S.3d 96, 101 (App. Div. 1st Dep't 2015); *Nussenzweig v. diCorcia*, 11 Misc. 3d 1051(A) (N.Y. Cty. 2006), *aff'd*, 38 A.D.3d 339 (1st Dep't), *certified question answered, order aff'd*, 9 N.Y.3d 184 (2007); *Lohan v. Perez*, 924 F. Supp. 2d 447 (E.D.N.Y. 2013) (Lindsay Lohan again, this time suing Pitbull); *Hoepker v. Kruger*, 200 F. Supp. 2d 340, 349 (S.D.N.Y. 2002).

Doe v. TCI Cablevision[53] is the suit of hockey player Tony Twist, then of the St. Louis Blues, against comic artist and entrepreneur, Todd McFarlane, creator of the *Spawn* comic. McFarlane is a hockey fan and St. Louis Blues fan, and decided to link his passions by creating a character in *Spawn* called Antonio Twistelli, who goes by nickname, "Tony Twist" (now you see the lawsuit issue). Another connection was that hockey's Tony Twist was known as a tough guy, an "enforcer" in hockey parlance, who goes out and levels "hits" on people who intentionally bump the star scorers of the team. So, too, was "Tony Twist" in *Spawn*: he was a gangster tough guy, also referred to as an "enforcer" in the comic. McFarlane went farther and included references to Tony Twist the hockey player in promotional activities for the comic, including a reference on a subscription solicitation page. This added to the commercialization allegations against McFarlane's use of Tony Twist's name and attributes of his persona.

[53] *Doe v. TCI Cablevision*, 110 S.W.3d 363 (Mo. 2003).

Hockey's Tony Twist, in St. Louis Blues uniform[54]

Spawn's Tony Twist, created by Todd McFarlane[55]

Twist sued, under a John Doe name, and named one of McFarlane's businesses as the first-named defendant. (Perhaps Twist didn't want McFarlane to get publicity value from being sued by a famous—or infamous—hockey player?) The court had to determine if the creative artistic expression of the comic and the nominal convergence of the two Tony Twist names were permitted under the Missouri right of publicity law (which was a court-developed, common law right in Missouri), as balanced by the First Amendment right of free speech and artistic expression. The court had its choice of the fair use tests used in *Cardtoons*, *Rogers*, *Comedy III*,

[54] Thumbnail-size excerpt of photograph of John Doe, a.k.a. Tony Twist, the plaintiff in *Doe v. TCI Cablevision*, 110 S.W.3d 363 (Mo. 2003).

[55] Thumbnail-size excerpt of cover art of the *Spawn* Comic, featuring the character, Tony Twist, at issue in *Doe v. TCI Cablevision*, 110 S.W.3d 363 (Mo. 2003).

Simeonov, and a few other, lesser-known cases. It decided to invent one of its own: the "predominant purpose test."[56]

The predominant purpose test looks at the nature of the expression, its content, its depth, and, to some extent, its value, and compares that to the nature of the use of the celebrity name, image, or likeness, and the commercialized advertising, merchandising, or other aspects of exploitation of the image or name, and makes a determination as to whether the use is more expressive than exploitative (fair use), or more exploitative of the celebrity's publicity than expressive (not fair use).[57]

It is difficult to articulate how this test differs from the *Cardtoons*' balancing test, but the court in *Doe* considered *Cardtoons* and still determined to write its test this way. The test is cognizant of the First Amendment public policies at work in this area, but also cognizant of the fact that some uses (such as McFarlane's) may start out as heavy artistic expression, and thus fair, but are dragged into commercialization and greater and greater exploitation, making them seem decidedly unfair. Yes, it is a sliding scale, and yes, it has all the unpredictability of a balancing test, but for the Missouri Supreme Court, it supplied the right analysis of the competing policies of this issue.

---

[56] *Doe*, 110 S.W.3d at 374 (quoting Mark S. Lee, *Agents of Chaos: Judicial Confusion in Defining the Right of Publicity-Free Speech Interface*, 23 LOY. L.A. ENT. L. REV. 471, 500 (2003)).

[57] *Id.*

Missouri had a follow-up case that wound up being litigated in the federal courts associated with Missouri, namely the Eastern District of Missouri trial level court, and the Eighth Circuit United States Court of Appeals. The case was *C.B.C. Distribution and Marketing, Inc. v. Major League Baseball Advanced Media, L.P.*[58] The CBC case is about fantasy baseball, but instead of a small-time fantasy league run among your buddies who gather around a ping pong table in your rec room, CBC is a for-profit service that supplies a lot of value for your fantasy team experience. The Major League Baseball Advanced Media people took note of it, and complained that the CBC package included small thumbnail images, names, and especially vital and professional statistics of major league baseball players that are vital to planning, managing, drafting, and trading the players on fantasy teams. The court of appeals looked to Missouri law, and found the *Doe* case and its predominant purpose test. The court of appeals had the benefit of other cases on baseball and the right of publicity,[59] and found that the publication of baseball news and statistics generally has been protected as a public interest kind of news and speech. Baseball is the national pastime, sayeth the courts, so the distribution of information about players and what they do is an important First Amendment protected activity. The details of identifying players by name and thumbnail image

---

[58] *C.B.C. Distribution & Mktg., Inc. v. Major League Baseball Advanced Media, L.P.*, 505 F.3d 818 (8th Cir. 2007).

[59] *E.g., Gionfriddo v. Major League Baseball*, 114 Cal. Rptr. 2d 307, 310 (Ct. App. 2001).

was regarded as incidental to the overall public interest in baseball activities. The for-profit nature of the enterprise did not doom it. The court balanced the factors on both sides and found that the predominant purpose was expressive and communicative of important public interest information, and was not predominantly exploitative of the players and their personae.[60]

TWO TESTS, NOT FIVE

Although the courts have not attempted to reconcile the purported differences between fair use tests, and instead treat publicity fair use law like a buffet from which any court can choose any number of different tests, in fact the five purported fair use tests overlap in substance and policy, and can be grouped into two tests:

(1) Relatedness—Predominant Purpose—Artistic Expression—Balancing Tests are all the same test, to evaluate the purpose behind the use of the celebrity name/image/likeness and its context and connection to the activity (i.e., high value expression or high commercial activity) to see if the use looks expressive and communicative or exploitative. Works that have high expressive value and are not commercial speech and not overtly

[60] *C.B.C.*, 505 F.3d at 824. As noted in Chapter 5, one of the latest cases to protect the publication of names, images, and statistics of sports players (college athletes) in connection with a for-profit fantasy league was *Daniels v. FanDuel, Inc.*, 109 N.E.3d 390, 397 (Ind. 2018) (answering certified question re: newsworthiness exception), 909 F.3d 876, 878 (7th Cir. 2018) (affirming dismissal of suit).

commercialized will be considered fair even when they feature the name, image, or likeness of a celebrity. Works that are highly commercialized in nature or in context and seek to exploit the celebrity's persona for gain in a fairly obvious manner will be considered unfair.

(2) Transformative Test is its own test, to weigh the speech/expression value added by the use through "transformation," or added to the endeavor by the valuable celebrity power of the artist herself. These two features of the transformative test do not overlap the features of the four other tests.

PICKING AND CHOOSING: APPLICATION OF FAIR USE TESTS IN PUBLICITY CASES

As noted above, courts have a distinct tendency to ignore the similarities and differences between fair use tests, and instead treat publicity fair use law like a buffet from which any court can choose any number of different tests in its fair use analysis. Over the years, *Rogers*' relatedness test and *Comedy III*'s transformative test have grown to be the most popular tests affording protection to both publicity interests and First Amendment artistic expression concerns. *Cardtoons* continues to be cited and discussed, but it has not been followed in making the ultimate determination of whether a use is fair or not in many years.[61] *Simeonov* gets mentioned in cases

---

[61] *ETW Corp.*, 332 F.3d at 915, worked through the analysis under the *Cardtoons*' test, but also applied the *Rogers*' Relatedness Test and *Comedy III*'s Transformative Test. *C.B.C.*, 505 F.3d at 822–24, also cited and discussed the *Cardtoons*' test, but

that involve fine arts, but it rarely has been used outside of New York State, and never as the sole test of fair use. *Doe* and *CBC* are used less often than the tests from *Rogers* and *Comedy III*, but they are cited from time to time.[62] The important take-away from this discussion is that courts, no matter where they are located, rarely pick one test and run with it. Instead, courts treat the tests as a buffet where they can have a little of this test, run a little analysis through a different test, and ultimately finish up with a run through of a third test.[63] If this sounds confusing, then you are understanding the situation correctly. The state of the law is as disjointed as it ever has been, and things are not likely to get much better in a "predictability of outcome" sense until one test becomes the norm in right of publicity situations.

PARKS V. LAFACE RECORDS[64]

Rosa Parks, the civil rights pioneer, was not pleased when the hip hop band, OutKast, used her name as a song title. The band, whose works are distributed by the first named defendant, LaFace Records, had written a song whose lyrics instructed upstart, newbie rappers and hip hop artists to "go to the back of the bus," which apparently, in OutKast's eyes,

---

ultimately applied the Predominant Purpose Test from *Doe*, 110 S.W.3d at 374.

[62] *Hart*, 717 F.3d at 151, cited and discussed the Predominant Purpose Test from *Doe*, 110 S.W.3d at 374, but ultimately settled on the Transformative test. (*Hart* is further discussed *infra*, Chapter 10).

[63] *Hart*, 717 F.3d at 151–54.

[64] *Parks v. LaFace Records*, 329 F.3d 437 (6th Cir. 2003).

called for the application of Ms. Parks' name as being someone famously associated with a request to move to the back of a bus. The court sympathized with Parks, not OutKast, but faced a dilemma of how to make the case come out in her favor. The court decided to apply two tests—*Cardtoons* and *Rogers*. Under *Cardtoons*,[65] the court found little value to the lyrics of the song, especially as they were (un)connected to Ms. Parks. The song was not about civil rights, or Birmingham, Alabama, or busing, or Ms. Parks at all. Thus, it had a hard time balancing out the exploitation potential of a prominent use of her famous name. The hip hop artists did not add new value to the work either by dint of artistic embellishments to the original (quantity of alteration being regarded as more important than quality). The court failed to note that the group brought to the table OutKast's, the artist's, own fame, and to their buying and listening public the market value of the artist's name, OutKast, is at least equal in importance to a civil rights figure from the 1950s. In either case, the end result was that the Rosa Parks name's publicity value was not overwhelmed by the new context of appearing on a hip hop album as a song title.

[65] *Id.* at 446, 448, 449, 459–60.

The court last considered the *Rogers v. Grimaldi* test,[66] and the court thought that this test was the most apt for the circumstances. It considered: (1) artistic relevance of the use of the name, Rosa Parks, in the context of the work, and (2) whether it appeared that the use of the name might "explicitly mislead" viewers or listeners as to the source or the content of the work. This test, and the way the court framed the application of the two criteria, did not favor OutKast. As mentioned above, the song itself had nothing to do with Rosa Parks or the events and history that she represented. The song title and prominent placement on the covers of the single release of the song placed the OutKast release on shelves of record stores alongside other albums of civil rights era music that Parks actually endorsed,

---

[66] *Id.* at 448–59, 460–61.

thus giving the band a lot of "stop and look at our album" value, as well as giving a competitive edge on albums that Parks herself endorsed. This worked out to be a case of disguised advertisement and exploitation, as opposed to protected expression.[67]

ETW CORP. V. JIREH PUB.[68]

ETW v. Jireh[69] was already discussed in Chapters 5 and 8 above. The case was decided by the same court (the Sixth Circuit) in the same week as *Parks*. The court applied many of the same tests to determine fair use. This time, the court was pleased with the expression evident in Rick Rush's art work.[70] The court found that Rush had provided worthwhile commentary on the sports and historical interest value of the Tiger Woods Masters tournament victory, thus giving him strong weights to throw into the scale on *Cardtoons* balancing. Rush prevailed on the balancing test. The court found that his entire effort to depict and describe the historical events revolved around the name, image, and likeness of Tiger, so the relatedness test of *Rogers* was satisfied in Rush's favor. And the court applied the *Comedy III* transformative test, and found that Rush's artistic treatment, additions, and embellishments (the multiple images, the backdrop, the addition of Butler Cabin, the addition of ghostly images of past

---

[67] *Id.* at 460–61.

[68] *ETW Corp. v. Jireh Pub., Inc.*, 332 F.3d 915 (6th Cir. 2003).

[69] Reduced-size excerpt of Rick Rush, *The Masters of Augusta*, the painting at issue in *ETW Corp. v. Jireh Pub., Inc.*, 332 F.3d 915 (6th Cir. 2003).

[70] *ETW*, 332 F.3d at 922–23.

champions, the addition of the famous leader board) all combined to sufficiently transform the image of Tiger in a manner that allowed Rush to prevail on that test, too. The result: fair use victory for Rick Rush.[71]

HOEPKER V. KRUGER[72]

Artist Barbara Kruger was sued when she used a work by German photographer, Thomas Hoepker, titled "Charlotte, as seen by Thomas." The work had been in the public domain in the United States, but it had been restored to copyright status by changes in U.S. law to accommodate our international obligations.[73] The publicity issue came not from

---

[71] *Id.*

[72] *Hoepker v. Kruger*, 200 F. Supp. 2d 340 (S.D.N.Y. 2002).

[73] *See* 17 U.S.C. § 104A; *Hoepker*, 200 F. Supp. 2d at 345.

Hoepker, but from Charlotte—as in Charlotte Dabney—the model who appears in the work. She objected to appearing in a Barbara Kruger work known as, *It's a small world but not if you have to clean it.*[74]

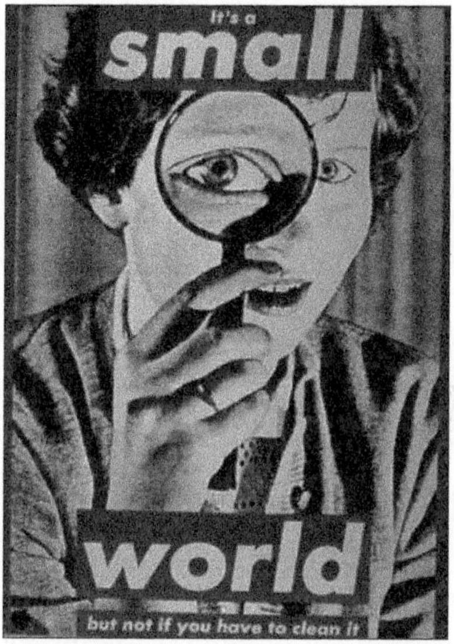

Kruger asserted a fair use defense to Dabney's right of publicity claims. As per usual in right of publicity cases, the court applied more than one test. *Simeonov* was a no-brainer under New York law—Kruger created an artistic rendition of a celebrity's image. That adds up to fair use under *Simeonov*'s artistic

[74] Reduced-size excerpt of Barbara Kruger's *It's a small world but not if you have to clean it*, the painting at issue in the case, *Hoepker v. Kruger*, 200 F. Supp. 2d 340 (S.D.N.Y. 2002).

expression test.[75] The court also used *Cardtoons'* balancing test which balanced in Kruger's favor; her strong artistic expression over-balanced an incidental exploitation of a thirty-year-old photograph of a model showing her appearance thirty years ago. The court also applied the *Comedy III* transformative test, and found that Kruger's creative additions transformed the original image of the celebrity, and also, on the subsidiary inquiry, that Kruger is well known for these artistic constructions of older photographs with new, ironic wording, so it would be very likely that people would collect the piece because it was a "Kruger" not because someone named Charlotte Dabney was seen in it.[76] All of these tests added up to a fair use victory for Kruger.

KIRBY V. SEGA OF AMERICA, INC.[77]

In *Kirby v. Sega of America, Inc.*, the California Court of Appeals evaluated the alleged use of a singer's image in a video game. Kierin Kirby, better known as Lady Miss Kier, the lead singer of the *Deee-Lite* band, brought a Lanham Act claim, right of publicity claim, misappropriation of likeness claim, and unfair competition claim against Sega for using her likeness. Kirby alleged that her look, which combines "retro and futuristic" styles, was unique. A character in Sega's video game, *Space Channel 5,* allegedly was based on her likeness. The character, Ulala, had a

---

[75] *Hoepker*, 200 F. Supp. 2d at 349, 351, 352.

[76] *Hoepker*, 200 F. Supp. 2d at 349–51.

[77] *Kirby v. Sega of Am., Inc.*, 50 Cal. Rptr. 3d 607 (Ct. App. 2006).

name that apparently mimicked the lyrics of *Groove is in the Heart*, which generally is recognized as *Deee-Lite*'s most famous song, and that has an "Oo-la-la" lyric that is sung by Kirby.[78]

Kirby (left) and Ulala (right)

Sega looked as if it were up to something, because the entertainment and toy company had approached Kirby in 2000 to see if she was interested in her hit single being used on their European version of the

[78] Thumbnail-size excerpt depicting Kierin Kirby, better known as Lady Miss Kier, and thumbnail-size excerpt depicting the Sega video game character, Ulala, the subjects of the case, *Kirby v. Sega of Am., Inc.*, 50 Cal. Rptr. 3d 607 (Ct. App. 2006).

game, but Kirby refused. The court held that the video game use of the celebrity likeness was transformative and therefore merited First Amendment protection.[79] The case was remanded to determine attorney's fees for Sega, as California law requires the prevailing party in such a claim to receive fees and costs.

ROMANTICS V. ACTIVISION PUB., INC.[80]

Activision's *Guitar Hero* and *Band Hero* franchises attracted another lawsuit in 2008, which had a similar outcome as *Kirby*. In *Romantics v. Activision*, the music group, *The Romantics*, complained under the Michigan right of publicity law regarding the use of the band's name, *The Romantics*, that popped up at the bottom of the screen in association with the use of one of the band's songs, *That's What I Like About You,* in the popular rock-and-roll simulation game, *Guitar Hero*. The game's creator, Activision, licensed the use of the song but did not license any of the band's or band members' publicity rights. But Activision did *not* display in the game the images, likenesses, or voices of the band members. Only the band's name showed up when the song was selected.

The band claimed Activision was exploiting their image and popularity because the group was so intimately associated with this song. The band alleged, in effect, that this was their "trademark" and signature song, and thus they claimed exploitation

---

[79] *Kirby*, 50 Cal. Rptr. 3d at 613–18.

[80] *Romantics v. Activision Pub., Inc.*, 574 F. Supp. 2d 758 (E.D. Mich. 2008).

when their name was displayed in the game in the phrase, "as made famous by The Romantics," that was displayed when the song was selected. The court found there was no right of publicity claim surviving beyond the copyrights to the lyrics and music which had been licensed to Activision. Further, even if a right of publicity claim survived, the court found that the First Amendment would allow the use of the name, *The Romantics*, to be associated with Activision' use of the song because the use in a video game was creative, expressive, and artistic, and the display of the band's name related directly to the content of the work.[81]

A FEW PARTING WORDS ON FAIR USE

Aside from news reporting, parody remains as the most appropriate, non-actionable use of famous celebrities' names and images.[82] Artists and their counsel should be wary of using images taken of unsuspecting persons taken on a city street. The

---

[81] *Id.* at 763–66.

[82] *See Winter*, 69 P.3d at 473, 480 (anthropomorphic portrayal of singers as half-worm beings was parody and non-actionable under Comedy III test); *World Wrestling Fed. Entm't, Inc. v. Big Dog Holdings, Inc.*, 280 F. Supp. 2d 413 (W.D. Pa. 2003) (anthropomorphic portrayal of WWF wrestling stars as dogs was parody and non-actionable).

results of disputes over such acquisitions of images is varied.[83]

[83] *Compare Nieves v. Home Box Office, Inc.*, 817 N.Y.S.2d 227 (App. Div. 1st Dep't 2006) (complaint of person filmed on street and used in bounty hunter reality TV show stated a claim), *and Mendonsa v. Time Inc.*, 678 F. Supp. 967 (D.R.I. 1988) (male subject of famous Eisenstadt photograph on V-J Day of a sailor kissing a dental assistant in New York City's Times Square stated claim for misappropriation of his image), *with Nussenzweig v. diCorcia*, 832 N.Y.S.2d 510 (App. Div. 1st Dep't 2007) (summary judgment awarded to street photographer who used close-up image of head of man taken on city street).

CHAPTER 10

THE FUTURE OF THE RIGHT OF PUBLICITY

In the future, the following scenario may occur more and more frequently in right of publicity disputes: the regulation of publicity rights if you create new performances with an old persona of a deceased artist. Modern digitalization and 3D computer-generated imagery (CGI) animation techniques allow artists and technicians to create new performances using the images and motion-captured or prior-recorded performances of deceased artists. Several well-known stars have performed in works after their deaths through the technology of CGI: Carrie Fisher in *Star Wars, Episode 9: The Rise Of Skywalker*; Peter Cushing in *Rogue One: A Star Wars Story*; Oliver Reed in *Gladiator*; Laurence Olivier in *Sky Captain and the World of Tomorrow*; and Marlon Brando in *Superman Returns*; to name but a few of the biggest names in acting after death. With the likely future development of advanced artificial intelligence, CGI recreations and even robotic humanoid avatars may become spontaneous and interactive players in creative works or the Metaverse,[1] moving far beyond any gimmickry that creates post-mortem cameo appearances in motion pictures, or places cherished stars in new

[1] The Metaverse is the term to describe the forthcoming Web 3.0 world of immersive experiences that will involve virtual reality and augmented reality. Within the Metaverse, avatars of visitors could watch or interact with digitally recreated versions of living or deceased celebrities.

advertisements for products whose producers would like to associate with the beloved former stars.

Tupac Shakur, who was killed in 1996, was "resurrected" in a virtual sort of way for a performance at Coachella in 2012.[2] The discussion began (or at least was "revived") about creations of new performances of deceased artists. Assuming you have the right footage or actual 3D digitalized files on hand, and you own or license the copyright to create derivative works from the source material, you can create new performances from pre-recorded source material. The question then is, can you create new virtual performances without the consent of the heirs of the performers?

[2] Thumbnail-size excerpt of a still taken from the video recording of Tupac Shakur virtually performing at the Coachella Concert in 2012 (2014).

The potential rights of publicity of the stars appearing in the earlier works that would serve as source material for new works may be preempted by the copyright over the source material. The technology for this kind of recreated performance exists. The actual performance of Tupac at Coachella used a modernized version of technology from the Nineteenth Century called Pepper's Ghost, which used reflective on-stage screens and below the stage mirrors on which images were projected to produce the appearance of a "live on-stage" performance.[3]

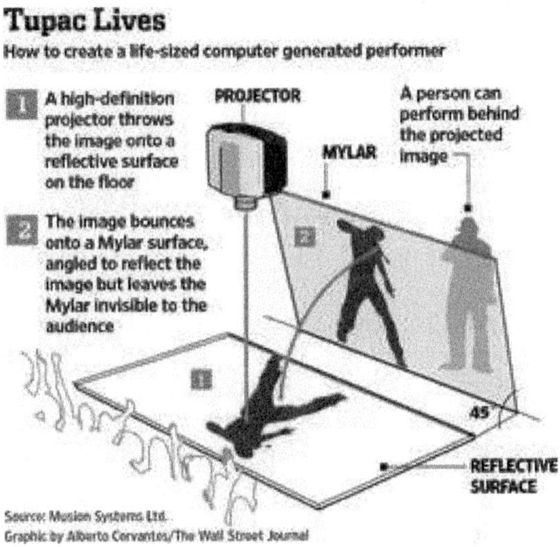

---

3 Thumbnail-size excerpt of diagram depicting the modern version of the *Pepper's Ghost Illusion*, used at the Coachella 2012 concert to allow the virtual performance of the deceased Tupac Shakur; Original Source: Musion Systems Ltd; Original Graphic by Alberto Cervantes for the Wall Street Journal (2012).

A recreated performance potentially violates the right of publicity of a deceased artist, but the artist's estate must be domiciled in a state that recognizes and enforces the post-mortem right of publicity. As discussed in Chapter 6, five states do not protect a right of publicity after death,[4] and nineteen others (including the District of Columbia) have not specified a term for the post-mortem right.[5]

But for the states that have a clearly defined post-mortem right, there remains the issue of whether the right of publicity is implicated by a recreated performance of a deceased celebrity. This seems to have an easy answer, too: "Yes," the posthumous right of publicity, if it exists in the state of the deceased's estate, is implicated by this blatant use of the artist's image, voice, performance style, and persona. The technology recreates almost 100% of the desirable qualities of the experience of the artist's performance, much more than the mere sound of the singing voice in *Midler*,[6] the sound of the speaking voice in *Facenda*,[7] and the single tag-line in *Carson*.[8] Note that the technology allows the creation of new

---

[4] Alaska, North Dakota, and Wyoming have no right of publicity, and Rhode Island and Wisconsin have no post-mortem right of publicity. Louisiana's right is limited to deceased soldiers. *See* Chapter 6 *supra*.

[5] Colorado, Connecticut, Delaware, District of Columbia, Idaho, Iowa, Kansas, Maine, Maryland, Minnesota, Mississippi, Missouri, Montana, New Hampshire, New Mexico, North Carolina, Oregon, Vermont, and West Virginia. *See id.*

[6] *Midler v. Ford Motor Co.*, 849 F.2d 460 (9th Cir. 1988).

[7] *Facenda v. N.F.L. Films, Inc.*, 543 F.3d 1007 (3d Cir. 2008).

[8] *Carson v. Here's Johnny Portable Toilets*, 698 F.2d 831 (6th Cir. 1983).

performances, it is not just a new and fun way to reshow recorded performances. Therefore, seeking the consent of the heirs or others who control the estate of the deceased artist is a very good idea. (This occurred with Tupac—his mother, the administrator of his estate, approved of the Coachella virtual performance).

As a fair use, the creation of new, virtual performances that replicate almost 100% of the creative, valuable, desirable attributes of the artist's persona when living is a technological achievement, but it is difficult to make a prediction as to whether it would be evaluated as transformative. On the one hand, the whole idea is to reproduce as much of the creative, valuable, desirable attributes of the artist's performances when living as you can. Success means that viewers are fooled into believing that the artist herself, in full persona, is really there, performing, just the way she used to, in front of their very eyes. That is near exact duplication, not transformation. It is not a new rapper compiled by manipulation of samples of several other rappers in a new composite. No, it is the one and only Tupac Shakur—or as close to the real Tupac as the technicians can get.

On the other hand, digital reanimation is nothing like any other depiction or reproduction of the image or likeness of a celebrity that we have ever seen before. Digital reanimation creates an entirely new context with completely new expression of the celebrity. Under a copyright law transformative test analysis, the recontextualization and addition of completely new content, meaning, and expression, which potentially could be employed for a completely new function and purpose, all might add up to a finding that the new works were transformative and a fair use. But right of publicity is different from copyright, and the new work still shows the celebrity for all of what the celebrity was famous for.

All of the rest of the potential commercial exploitation of the celebrity's name, image, and persona exists, too—the concert promotions, the new recordings, the new music videos, the potential tie-in to other product promotions—all of which would affect the relatedness-balancing-predominant purpose tests of *Rogers*, *Cardtoons*, and *Doe* in a non-fair use direction. Potentially, all of our deceased film stars and other performers could virtually appear in new films. Remember that the technology does not just recontextualize old Tupac footage into a 2012 concert with Snoop Dog (Snoop Lion) and others. It is a new experience of Tupac's persona.

The copyright preemption issue arises if the person doing the creation of new, virtual performances owns or licenses the copyrights to the records of the performer's appearances and performances that were used to create the new, virtual performances. Only a small part of this question has been answered in cases such as *Midler*, *Waits*, and *Facenda* that dealt with musical compositions and a prerecorded voice track—if new works are created beyond the copyrighted material that is licensed, and the new works mimic or replicate protected aspects of the celebrity's persona (such as the sound of their voice), then the new works might violate the celebrity's right of publicity. But if an entire audio or audio-visual recording is the material in question, and the material is used by the owner or licensee of the copyright to the material to create derivatives of the same nature as the original—new musical recordings derived from original musical recordings, and new motion picture footage derived from original motion picture footage—then it would seem that copyright preemption power might protect the creation of these derivative works, and preempt the right of publicity of the stars appearing and performing in the original recorded works.

Some guidance may be found in recent litigation by collegiate football players seeking to enforce their publicity against the maker of football simulation video games. Like the scenario of CGI animated acting that produces new "performances," sports-simulation video games are used to stage new, virtual contests between avatars of real players. The video game does not simply replay college football games in virtual 3D, it allows the creation of new games, games that never happened and in which the players never participated.

In a pair of cases, *Hart v. Electronic Arts*,[9] and *In re NCAA Student-Athlete Name & Likeness Licensing Litigation*,[10] the courts considered the rights of student athletes to control their images and

---

[9] *Hart v. Electronic Arts*, 717 F.3d 141, 165–70 (3d Cir. 2013).

[10] *In re NCAA Student-Athlete Name & Likeness Licensing Litig.*, 724 F.3d 1268 (9th Cir. 2013), *aff'g*, *Keller v. Elecs. Arts, Inc.*, No. C 09–1967 CW, 2010 WL 530108, at *1 (N.D. Cal. Feb. 8, 2010).

likenesses when the students' sports league, the NCAA, had licensed all of the other intellectual property associated with college football—the names of the teams, the uniforms, the team logos, the fight songs, the appearance of the stadiums, and much more—to EA Sports, the manufacturer of the football simulation games.

In *Hart*, the District Court for the District of New Jersey noted that NCAA student athletes were not permitted to license and profit from their actual identities as players under strictly enforced NCAA rules. The student athletes could not sell their own jerseys or sell autographs or engage in other commercial activities relating to their athletic endeavors. This undercut the logic of the suit severely; it seemed that even if the rest of their complaint stated a cause of action for violations of publicity rights, there were no functional damages. The game maker also successfully alleged fair uses in defense of the suit, the most important of which was that the game was transformative. Hart's suit was dismissed, and the *Hart* case went up on appeal.

On appeal, the United States Court of Appeals for the Third Circuit carefully examined whether defendant EA Sports was entitled to the First Amendment defense recognized by the District Court. The Third Circuit reviewed three of the prevailing fair use tests: the predominant purpose test (*Doe*, *CBC* test), the relatedness test (*Rogers* test), and the transformative test (*Comedy III* test), and determined that the transformative test from California state law was the most apt for the situation of Hart's case.

The Third Circuit painstakingly broke down the issue of the strong First Amendment protection for expressive media such as video games, and the meaning and application of the transformative test. In spite of the completely different meaning, purpose, context, and message, and the transformation from a real life player in actual football games to a completely fanciful, visual recreation in a digital virtual reality of a computerized football simulation game, the Court made the remarkable observation that there was no real difference between a depiction of Hart the actual football player in actual football games, and the avatar appearance of Quarterback No. 13 for Rutgers in the football simulation computer game. EA Sports had not made sufficient change in "context, meaning, and expression" from the actual Hart's appearance to the avatar in the video game to justify the label of transformation and the fair use protection that goes with the label.

The issue in *NCAA Athletes Name & Likeness Licensing Litigation* was framed differently, because the court had to respond to a motion by EA Sports that the entire lawsuit was a "Strategic lawsuit against public participation" (SLAPP) under California's anti-SLAPP statute—meaning that the only reason for the suit was to put pressure on EA Sports to cease exercising its free expression rights, which it typically exercised by making and selling video games. The District Court denied the motion for the somewhat unusual reasoning that the motion was improper because EA Sports did not have First Amendment rights and protections in the video game that would need to be protected in the anti-SLAPP motion. This signaled that the lawsuit of the athletes had merit and was not just a bullying technique to "quiet" the video game maker's speech. And the reason the suit had merit was that EA Sports did not enjoy a transformative fair use (*Comedy III* test) over the images of the athletes. The Ninth Circuit agreed and affirmed the case on appeal.

In essence, the Ninth Circuit opinion followed *Hart*: it agreed that the transformative test was the superior test (it considered the relatedness test of *Rogers*, too), and it found that the treatments of the athletes' images were not transformative. The lawsuit only represents a disposition on the anti-SLAPP motion to dismiss, but the ruling indicates that the athletes' claims have merit and are likely to succeed, so it telegraphs to the parties that EA Sports is not going to sail through the case on the strength of its First Amendment defenses.

In the entertainment field, there is enough of a question concerning use of existing recordings to create new performances that the topic of future and post-mortem creation and recreation of works using existing works should be negotiated and provided for in a musician's or actor's contract with the producers of the original works. If covered by contract, then it would be clear that the original owner has or does not have the right to use the original recorded appearances, sounds, and performances as the source material to make new digitalized, animated appearances and performances.

Copyright alone may not be enough to answer the right of publicity questions. The meaning and power of the new technology is in the creation of new, virtual appearances and performances that go far beyond the existing recordings. The idea is to give the audience the experience that that the performer really is present before them, doing something new. Strutting, dancing, singing, sweating—giving them an exposure to the star's persona, albeit by virtual means. That seems to go beyond the rights that copyright protects in *fixed*, tangible, existing works. *Facenda* sued and prevailed when the NFL wanted to make new voiceover "performances" using the sound of his voice as collected and recorded in existing copyrighted recordings of NFL Films. This was only one aspect of the John Facenda experience. With Tupac, the audience was treated to a much broader experience—a virtual performance of the man himself—that is not tied to one or even a dozen recorded and copyrighted performances. The whole persona of a performer is not easily captured in copyrightable recordings, and for that reason, the law might not allow copyright to preempt the assertion of separate rights of publicity of the estate of deceased artists and performers.

APPENDIX

CHART OF THE FIFTY STATES' RIGHT OF PUBLICITY LAWS

This chart reports the status of all fifty states and the District of Columbia as to the enactment of a statute regarding the right of publicity, or the adoption of a common law rule enforcing the right of publicity (Common law (publicity)) or a common law rule enforcing the "appropriation" tort under a right of privacy theory (Common Law (privacy)—*see* Chapter 3), and further reports whether the states' statutes or courts have addressed the issue of whether the rights will be enforced after death.

State	Statutory or Common Law Right	Post-Mortem Right, Term of Years
Alabama	Statute—Ala. Code § 6–5–770 et seq.	Yes—55 years
Alaska	None	None
Arizona	Common Law (publicity), and a statute for	Yes (term uncertain[1])

[1] Arizona, Georgia, Michigan, New Jersey, and South Carolina are marked "term uncertain" under Post-Mortem Rights because the states' courts have recognized a common law right of publicity, and the courts have indicated that the right will be enforced after death, but have not provided a term of years for the post-mortem right. Arizona's statute, Ariz. Rev. Stat. § 12–761, is limited to uses of soldiers' names, portraits, or pictures for commercial purposes, and it does not have a post-mortem limitations period.

State	Statutory or Common Law Right	Post-Mortem Right, Term of Years
	soldiers—Ariz. Rev. Stat. § 12–761	
Arkansas	Statute—Ark. Code § 4–75–1101 et seq.	Yes—50 years
California	Statute—Cal. Civ. Code §§ 3344, 3344.1	Yes—70 years
Colorado	Common Law (privacy)	Unknown[2]
Connecticut	Common Law (privacy)	Unknown[2]
Delaware	Common Law (privacy)	Unknown[2]
District of Columbia	Common Law (privacy)	Unknown[2]
Florida	Statute—Fla. Stat. § 540.08	Yes—40 years
Georgia	Common Law (publicity)	Yes (term uncertain[1])

[2] Colorado, Connecticut, Delaware, District of Columbia, Idaho, Iowa, Kansas, Maine, Maryland, Minnesota, Mississippi, Missouri, Montana, New Hampshire, New Mexico, North Carolina, Oregon, Vermont, and West Virginia are marked "unknown" as to post-mortem rights when the states' courts have only recognized a common law right of privacy or publicity, and the states' courts have not addressed the issue of whether the rights will be enforced after death.

State	Statutory or Common Law Right	Post-Mortem Right, Term of Years
Hawaii	Statute—Haw. Rev. Stat. § 482P–1 et seq.	Yes—70 years
Idaho	Common Law (privacy)	Unknown[2]
Illinois	Statute—765 Ill. Comp. Stat. 1075/1 et seq.	Yes—50 years
Indiana	Statute—Ind. Code § 32–36–1–0.2 et seq.	Yes—100 years
Iowa	Common Law (privacy)	Unknown[2]
Kansas	Common Law (privacy)	Unknown[2]
Kentucky	Statute—Ky. Rev. Stat § 391.170	Yes—50 years
Louisiana	Common Law (privacy), and a statute for deceased soldiers—La. Rev. Stat. § 14:102.21[3]	No (except for deceased soldiers[3])
Maine	Common Law (privacy)	Unknown[2]

[3] Louisiana has a criminal statute preventing the exploitation of a deceased soldier's name, portrait, or picture for commercial purposes. *See* La. Rev. Stat. § 14:102.21. Like Arizona's soldiers' statute, it has no specified term of years.

State	Statutory or Common Law Right	Post-Mortem Right, Term of Years
Maryland	Common Law (privacy)	Unknown[2]
Massachusetts	Statute—Mass. Gen. Laws ch. 214, §§ 1B, 3A	Unknown[4]
Michigan	Common Law (publicity)	Yes (term uncertain[1])
Minnesota	Common Law (publicity)	Unknown[2]
Mississippi	Common Law (privacy)	Unknown[2]
Missouri	Common Law (publicity)	Unknown[2]
Montana	Common Law (privacy)	Unknown[2]
Nebraska	Statute—Neb. Rev. Stat. § 20–201 et seq.	Unknown[4]
Nevada	Statute—Nev. Rev. Stat. § 597.770 et seq.	Yes—50 years
New Hampshire	Common Law (publicity)	Unknown[2]

[4] Massachusetts' statutes on privacy and publicity, Mass. Gen. Laws ch. 214, §§ 1B, 3A, Nebraska's statute on right of publicity, Neb. Rev. Stat. § 20–201 et seq., and Utah's statute on abuse of personal identity, Utah Code Ann. § 45–3–1 et seq., do not specify whether the rights apply after death, and no courts have addressed this issue.

State	Statutory or Common Law Right	Post-Mortem Right, Term of Years
New Jersey	Common Law (publicity)	Yes (term uncertain[1])
New Mexico	Common Law (publicity)	Unknown[2]
New York	Statute—N.Y. Civ. Rights Law §§ 50, 50–f, 51	Yes—40 years
North Carolina	Common Law (privacy)	Unknown[2]
North Dakota	None	None
Ohio	Statute—Ohio Rev. Code § 2741.01 et seq.	Yes—60 years
Oklahoma	Statute—Okla. Stat. tit. 12, §§ 1448, 1449	Yes—100 years
Oregon	Common Law (publicity)	Unknown[2]
Pennsylvania	Statute—42 Pa. Cons. Stat. § 8316	Yes—30 years
Rhode Island	Statute—R.I. Gen. Laws § 9–1–28	None
South Carolina	Common Law (publicity)	Yes (term uncertain[1])
South Dakota	Statute—S.D. Codified Laws § 21–64–1 et seq.	Yes—70 years

State	Statutory or Common Law Right	Post-Mortem Right, Term of Years
Tennessee	Statute—Tenn. Code Ann. § 47–25–1101	Yes—10 years or unlimited if still used[5]
Texas	Statute—Tex. Prop. Code Ann. § 26.001 et seq. (applies to deceased persons); Common Law (publicity) right applies to living persons	Yes—50 years
Utah	Statute—Utah Code Ann. § 45–3–1 et seq.	Unknown[4]
Vermont	Common Law (privacy)	Unknown[2]
Virginia	Statute—Va. Code Ann. § 8.01–40	Yes—20 years
Washington	Statute—Wash. Rev. Code § 63.60.010 et seq.	Yes—10 years (for "individuals") but 75 years (for "personalities,"

[5] Tennessee's statute, Tenn. Code Ann. § 47–25–1104, provides an initial term of ten years, but the right remains in effect if continuously used after the ten year term. The right will be terminated by proof of non-use for two years.

State	Statutory or Common Law Right	Post-Mortem Right, Term of Years
		if persona had value at death)
West Virginia	Common Law (publicity)	Unknown[2]
Wisconsin	Statute—Wis. Stat. § 995.50	None
Wyoming	None	None

INDEX

References are to Pages